Terry Wogan, one of Bri
alities, was born in Limeri   , and grew up in Dublin. He
joined the Royal Bank of Ireland, where he was a clerk for five
years. It was then that he saw an advertisement in the local paper
for a newsreader/announcer for Radio Eireann, applied for the
job, and was chosen from among 2,500 applicants. He progressed
to become one of Ireland's most popular TV and radio person-
alities. According to one reporter he was a 'sort of matinée idol,
circa 1963'. By 1967 he was ready to move on and sent a tape to
the BBC, who invited him to present *Late Night Extra*. He in-
itially commuted to London by plane, but in 1969 he and his family moved to England. Shortly afterwards he was asked to stand in
for Jimmy Young and was given a regular afternoon slot as a
result. In 1972 he took over the breakfast show on Radio 2 and
quickly evolved his own style – trading insults with his listeners,
making irreverent introductions to records and fellow DJ's – a
constant stream of good-natured 'badinage' and 'calumny'.

As well as his work for radio he compèred several television
shows, including *Come Dancing*. His major television break-
through came in 1979 with *Blankety Blank*, which regularly topped
the TV ratings. In 1982 his career took a new turn when he was
offered his own 'live' show, entitled *Wogan*. The programme established him as the country's top TV chat-show host and, since
1985, has been screened 'live' three times a week.

From the late seventies onwards, Terry Wogan has won virtu-
ally every poll for 'Most Popular TV Personality'. In 1982 he received the prestigious Pye Award for Radio Personality of the
Year and in 1985 won the Variety Club of Great Britain Award for
'Show Business Personality of the Year'. In 1988 he won the *TV
Times* 'TV Personality of the Year' award for the tenth year
running.

WOGAN
◄ON►
WOGAN

TERRY WOGAN

Edited by Peter Estall

PENGUIN BOOKS

PENGUIN BOOKS

Published by the Penguin Group
27 Wrights Lane, London W8 5TZ, England
Viking Penguin Inc., 40 West 23rd Street, New York, New York 10010, USA
Penguin Books Australia Ltd, Ringwood, Victoria, Australia
Penguin Books Canada Ltd, 2801 John Street, Markham, Ontario, Canada L3R 1B4
Penguin Books (NZ) Ltd, 182–190 Wairau Road, Auckland 10, New Zealand

Penguin Books Ltd, Registered Offices: Harmondsworth, Middlesex, England

First published by Robson Books 1987
Published in Penguin Books 1988
1 3 5 7 9 10 8 6 4 2

Made and printed in Great Britain by
Richard Clay Ltd, Bungay, Suffolk
Filmset in Times

Contents

Acknowledgements

First, I must say thank you to the 'Wogan' team, past and present, who have succoured my guests on Mondays, Wednesdays and Fridays, with a special thanks to my Series Producers Frances Whitaker and John Fisher, and to Producer Jon Plowman.

And of course to my guests themselves. Little did they know what was in store when they arrived, agog with excitement, at the BBC Television Theatre – and here they are in print!

Space unfortunately dictated leaving out so many of our guests – after all, we've had more than a thousand. Nothing was more difficult than deciding who to include . . . Those left out might well consider themselves the lucky ones . . .

To all the Wogan guests, sincerest thanks for their company and conversation. Without them, there might have been a lot of silence around Shepherd's Bush Green.

A word of thanks to the BBC is in order too, if only to make sure that we all hold on to our jobs.

Thank you also to Peter Estall, a producer on 'Wogan' since the beginning, who has been willing to undergo yet again the trauma of it all as we went through the videos of the shows trying to put this book together. Despite his masochistic tendencies, a man of sterling worth.

And finally, thank you to Dorothy Stewart, my editor with Robson, for her girlish sense of fun, and a lot of hard graft.

Introduction

PICTURE, IF YOU WILL, Shepherd's Bush Green on a
balmy summer's evening: The drowsy hum of the bee blend-
ing easily with the effortless song of blackbird, thrush and lark, the
noisy screech of the strutting peacock and the languid croak of the
bullfrog. Here the humming-bird flits noiselessly from bloom to
bloom, whilst the elegant flamingo stands motionless by the still
water. On every side hibiscus and the fragrant frangipani, the
blazing bougainvillea and the delicate orchid. And over all, the
gentle scent of mimosa and orange blossom . . .

Over there, on the corner, by the Bush Public House, with its
gay awnings, multi-coloured parasols and string quartet, is that
jewel in the diadem of architectural richness that is Shepherd's
Bush: the BBC Television Theatre. Let us go inside . . .

The smartly-dressed commissionaires, ex-guardsmen to a man,
and trained to a hair in the martial arts, greet us civilly and usher us
into what seems a maelstrom. For it is 6.30pm, and in a scant 30
minutes, 'Wogan' will be on the air! All is hustle and bustle:
Cheery-faced researchers rush hither and thither with last-minute
messages, and warming bowls of broth for the nervous guests;
make-up ladies make haste to provide the finishing touches to their
charges. On the stage, cameramen discuss earnestly with floor-
managers, sound-men adjust their booms, lighting-men scurry
about the gantries. The audience, already seated, whisper in awe,
their excitement and anticipation almost tangible. Above their
heads, in the control room, sober-minded producers do their best
to calm the mounting tension. The director paces restlessly, chain-
smoking, the vision-mixer flexes her supple fingers, the production

9

assistant rushes from the room for the third time in ten minutes . . .

Were we but able to look inside Dressing Room No.1, what a contrast would meet our eyes: The Great Man Himself steps lightly from his sunken bath with its subtle fragrances, into the softest of huge towels, held for him by one of several scantily-dressed lovelies. Another leads him to a chaise-longue, and with firm, yet caressing fingers kneads Our Hero's body with precious salves and unguents.

There is a knock on the dressing-room door. 'Fifteen minutes to transmission, Mr. Wogan!' shouts a nervous, respectful voice. Wordlessly, calmly, Wogan dismisses his lovely helpers, for he likes to spend the last few minutes before the show alone with his thoughts. As he dresses, he sips reflectively on his Louis Roederer Cristal, drawing ruminatively the while on a Davidoff Chateau Margaux. With five minutes to go, a sound operator requests admission and is admitted to the opulent dressing-room with its Persian carpets, Louis Quinze furniture and exquisite draperies. Apologetically, the man affixes a microphone to The Star's hand-woven silk tie.

Smiling and benevolent, with a word even for the lowliest warm-up man, He makes his way to the wings. The stage-hands greet Him with yeoman respect: 'Lord bless you, Guv'nor!', 'Good luck to your Honour!', 'Break a leg, Sir!' There is scarcely time for Wogan to scatter a few coins, before the familiar opening bars of His theme-tune strike up. With a rueful smile, The Great Man straightens his back and walks purposefully on-stage . . . Another 'Wogan' has begun . . .

'Wogan' – a Pen-Picture . . .

It is thought that Terry Wogan slipped through customs into Britain sometime in the late 1960s or early 1970s. He applied to BBC Radio for a job as a disc-jockey, claiming previous experience in broadcasting in Ireland. On investigation, nobody there had ever heard of him, least of all *Eamonn Andrews*, to whom he claimed to be related, on the tenuous grounds of 'a second cousin, twice removed'.

It is not known for certain how Wogan wormed his way into the studios and began broadcasting on Radios 1 and 2. David Hatch, Managing Director Radio, says: 'Nobody knows quite how he did it. We suspect he found an empty studio, switched on the microphone, and began to speak. The commissionaires have no powers to eject anyone from the building, so we just left him to it . . .'

In a very short time, Wogan had ingratiated himself with the two most powerful men in the BBC: *Tony Blackburn*, at whose jokes he always laughed first and longest, and *Jimmy Young*, whose wheel-chair he regularly serviced. Relentlessly, day in, day out, he broadcast through the long, weary afternoons on Radios 1 and 2, his 'Fight The Flab' exercise sessions wreaking havoc among the lumbar regions of Britain's hitherto healthy matrons.

As evidence of the danger he represented to the nation one example will suffice: One afternoon, Wogan had the impudence to suggest that a sovereign method of divining whether you were overweight or not was to take all your clothes off, and jump up and down in front of a mirror. Then, if anything bounced, that, as it were, wasn't designed for the purpose, you were overweight, and needed to lose the non-designer bouncing bits . . . Some weeks later a distressed listener wrote in to complain that, her husband having left for work, she retired to her boudoir, removed her clothes, and jumped up and down. Her husband, returning unexpectedly, had got the wrong end of the stick, removed *his* clothes, and now she was pregnant . . .

Shortly afterwards, Wogan overslept on one of the warm airducts on the pavement outside the BBC, and on running to his studio, found it barred and padlocked against him. His afternoon show was over. However, entering Broadcasting House the following morning before the canteen opened, he found the place deserted. It was for him the work of a moment to enter another empty studio. And so began the Breakfast Show . . .

We need not dwell here overlong on the excess and abuse that characterised the next 12 years: The attempted character assassination of the revered D.G.; the foul slurs on many senior executives; the twin canards of The Block on Promotion and Bloodstained Corridors; the bare-faced lies about lighthouses in Northampton, and Self-Propelling Cones on Motorways; the evil attempt to undermine the moral fibre of the nation by encouraging the people to bet on 'Wogan's Winner', which in turn led to the attempted 'Harnessing of Nameless Forces'!

By now crazed with fame, Wogan hit upon the idea of The Power of The Mind as a method of winning horse-races. He asked all his listeners to concentrate on a horse called 'Mrs. Penny' that was running in the 2.30 at Towcester. At 2.30 that very afternoon, millions of people were to stop what they were doing, and think hard of 'Mrs. Penny'. If there was anything to the Power of Thought, or Mind Over Matter, surely the brain-waves of millions of Britons would propel 'Mrs. Penny' past the finishing post with furlongs to spare over her rivals.

Two days later, a letter from a perplexed woman said that she had been walking down the High Street of the little town where she lived, when at 2.30 precisely, she had been picked up by some great, unseen hand and propelled at high speed for a mile and seven furlongs to the outskirts of the town, where, just as suddenly, the Force had left her. She signed herself 'Mrs. Penny' . . . the horse, of course, came nowhere . . .

Then too, there was the encouragement of Eccentricity Among The Populace: When a report in a newspaper said that a cross-channel swimmer had claimed to have fallen asleep on the job, Wogan felt constrained to point out that if the swimmer had indeed slept, he would surely have sunk to the bottom like a stone. Swimming and sleeping, Wogan pointed out his pedantic way, were two diametrically opposed activities. If you tried one while doing the other, nothing but ill could befall.

This was borne out by another missive, this time from a gentleman in Birmingham who, inspired by the tale of the sleeping swimmer, had the notion of challenging the might of the Channel while tied to a lamp-post. Unfortunately he had been apprehended by the Police halfway down the M1, covered in goose-grease and tied to the aforesaid lamp-post. They had been sceptical of his tale, and all he asked of Wogan was to send a message over the airwaves to his wife at Cap Gris Nez, where she was waiting with sandwiches and tea to sustain him for the return journey . . .

This kind of thing could not be allowed to last of course. Eventually a strong force of Executive Producers with *Bryant Marriot*, Controller Radio 2, at their head, succeeded in ejecting Wogan from his fortified studio, though not before he had inflicted some nasty flesh wounds with some well-directed Nolan Sisters records.

The problem was, Wogan knew where The Body Was Buried . . . Friend and confidant of tea-lady, commissionaire and duty-officer alike, he had amassed a wealth of secret detail and little known fact about the seedy goings-on in the corridors of power of the BBC. He was thought to be in possession of the only known recording of 'Pibroch of Donal Dhu' by a young, callow Alistair Milne. He had boasted of knowing the whereabouts of certain pictures of Michael Grade taken without his knowledge, or braces. He had letters written by Duke Hussey long before he was even a baronet. Something had to be done . . .

A solution was thrashed out in the boardroom of the BBC, over a bottle of perfectly filthy house claret and some very grey lamb cutlets, left over from the last governors' meeting. The meeting itself was heated, with the spirit of the sainted Lord Reith freely invoked, and candles lit before the portrait of Grace Wyndham Goldie. Old tapes of 'The Radio Doctor' and 'ITMA' were played, and a BBC insider reports that the Head of Light Entertainment Group (Television) was more than once reduced to uncontrollable sobbing . . .

Eventually, a decision was taken, in time-honoured BBC fashion: Since Wogan couldn't be fired, he should be promoted. 'Head of Outside Broadcasts, World Service' was a popular suggestion, on the grounds that it would keep Wogan out of the country for much of the year. 'Chief Announcer, Radio 3' was freely mooted on the basis that most of the population would think he was dead. He was even suggested as a presenter of 'Breakfast Time', on the same principle . . .

Then Bill Cotton, a left-handed golfer of some repute, had a bright idea: 'Let's give him a television chat-show! That'll soften his cough! We'll put him on three times a week at peak viewing-hour. He'll be dead in six weeks. If the work doesn't kill him, the tabloids will!' A unanimous shout of approbation greeted this cruel suggestion, and Cotton himself was immediately promoted to the sinecure position of 'Managing Director, Television' . . .

Wogan, of course, was no stranger to television. He had spent seven long, hard-fought years as the compere of 'Come Dancing', where, incidentally, he became better known under the pseudonym of 'The Beast of the Ballroom', but that's another story, and best left to stronger stomachs than yours, dear reader. Wogan travelled the length and breadth of the country, in his soup-stained dinner jacket, on a second-class rail ticket. His producer travelled first-class. In those days, the BBC had a short way with hobbledehoys and mummers – would that it were still the case today!

Without being able to put a foot under him, he had the crass nerve to introduce the Fylde Waltz, the Military Two-Step and the Paso-Doble from Glasgow to Purley, from Swansea to Hammersmith. He claimed the acquaintanceship of every formation team from Scarborough to Penge. Such was the impact of his stewardship of this fine programme that, after seven years, the British viewing public were still firmly convinced that it was being compered by the previous incumbent, Peter West.

As ever, alert to the writing on the D.G's loo wall, Wogan moved right along, this time to a heavily-intellectual quiz-show, 'Blankety-Blank'. This involved questions of a highly philosophical, scientific or theological nature, which were put first to members of the public (whose I.Q. could not be less than 175) and then to a panel of dons, professors and senior civil servants.

It quickly caught the public's imagination, probably because of the excellent prizes on offer: mug-trees, plastic bicycles, and weekends in Reykjavik. Wogan simply did not have the wit, weight or 'bottom' for it. He was soon replaced by the more serious minded lecturer, Les Dawson, whose definitive work on the Early Chinese Renaissance had caused such a stir in the groves of academe.

There was nothing on Wogan's broadcasting horizon, apart from the Eurovision Song Contest and the Variety Club Award, when he received that fateful phone-call from 'Sir' Michael Grade's third assistant footman: ' ' E wants to see you. Bring the money in used oncers . . .' Grade was in Los Angeles at the time, and Wogan made his way there by steam-packet and mule-train. Arriving at the young lion's plush apartment, just off Wilshire, Wogan knocked timidly at the great door. 'Enter!' commanded a surprisingly young voice. 'Oh, it's only you', he snarled, upon observing the sweat-stained presenter. 'What kept you? And why are you covered in sweat?' 'I walked' replied Wogan. 'You walked? *Walked*? Nobody here walks. In L.A. you pay people to walk *for* you . . .'

The rest of the acrimonious conversation, and the brief contractual discussion that followed ('Sign here! Now clear off!') is too well-documented in Bob Monkhouse's seminal work, 'Bob says, It's The BBC! 1980-1987!' to bear repetition here. Suffice it to say that in February 1985, Wogan began his eponymous thrice-weekly stint, and has proved extemely difficult to shake off, since. Through dungeon, fire and sword he has talked unsparingly with those foolish enough to sit down on his overstuffed and undersprung settee, and break conversational bread with him. He has chatted on trains, on golf courses, on roofs, on Holy Shepherd's Bush Green itself, and outside the front door in the rain.

By the time you read this, unless a merciful providence intervenes, he will have talked to well over a thousand guests from the Princess Royal to the Queens of Soap; from Luciano Pavarotti and Stephen Sondheim to Boy George and Frankie Goes To Hollywood; from Kirk Douglas to Michael J. Fox; from here to eternity . . . 'Let my people go!' is the cry, but Wogan shows no sign of flagging. Almost 400 live shows in the bag, but the boy won't quit . . .

For those of you of a similar frame of mind, this slim volume is

15

meekly offered. It's also, of course, for those of you who may foolishly have missed a fleeting moment or two on Mondays, Wednesdays and Fridays between 7 and 7.35pm on BBC 1 over the last three years. Shame on you! This is your chance to catch up. Pay attention now. We shall be asking questions later . . .

Stewart Granger

S TEWART GRANGER is a star whose personality fully
matches the image created by movies such as *King
Solomon's Mines* and *Beau Brummel*.

The first time he came on 'Wogan', he horrified me by
recounting some of the derring-do's that he had to perform to
earn an honest crust in the early days of Hollywood . . . the
days before his stuntmen took all the risks. In fact it was a
minor miracle that he was still here to tell the tales.

One of my narrowest escapes was when I was making a film with
Mel Ferrer called *Scaramouche*. They had dreamt up this scene
where I was fencing madly with Mel. He trips me and I was
supposed to fall over. As I fell, the idea was that an enormous
chandelier crashed to the ground just as I rolled out of the way.
The director took me through the scene.

He said 'It will be a lovely shot. See this hole in the ground.
You're lying in the front on a mattress, and the camera's in the
ground. And we see with the camera as if it's your eyes, we see the
chandelier come 'whoooo' like that, and it stops. It will be a
wonderful shot.'

I said 'Supposing it doesn't stop?' He looked amazed and said
'Jim, c'mon. This is MGM for goodness sake. We do this all the
time.'

I said 'I'd like to see it.' So this bored look came over the faces of
the crew. 'Oh all right. Let it go, Cyril.' (The special effects man
was Cyril).

Cyril let it go and it went whooooeeee - boom! Crash! It didn't stop. It buried itself into solid wood. The mattress I was supposed to lie on was absolutely hamburgered. I'd have been wiped out.

There was a deathly silence except for the sobbing of Cyril. 'Oh my God,' he wept, 'it's never happened before.' And the director was throwing up. I said 'Yes, interesting,' and I walked to my dressing room, and then I threw up!

Later on, with James Mason, there was a famous scene when I was up against the wall, and a man who was wonderful with the sword is coming right for my face. So I parried, and parried. He was a buddy of mine, so I said 'No, come right for my face', and I parried it, and parried it. And then I forgot to parry it the other way. 'Boom!' Right in my teeth. If steel hits your teeth, there's the most dreadful sound. And he was frozen. A look of horror came into his face. I could just about say 'Take the huhuh sword out of my mouth.' He took the sword out and blood just poured. He had gone right into my gum!

But the worst, or the bravest thing, I ever did was filming *Solomon's Mines*. I have a horror of snakes. And there was a scene where I was to work with a cobra. There's a feller called Alan Tarson who had this cobra - a wild cobra.

I said 'You're going to milk it (milk the venom out), aren't you?' He said 'Oh no, a cobra's not stupid. If you milk it, it won't throw its hood. It knows.'

I said 'What are you going to do?' 'Oh we'll tape its mouth, with Scotch Tape. It'll be alright.'

I noticed just before we did a 'take' that the snake tried to have a go at Alan. Then it's 'Action' and I come on and the snake comes up. I take my hat off, hit it and grab hold of it and shake it to make it angry. Then I pretend to take out my revolver and kill it. Then it's 'Cut, cut' followed by Alan shouting 'Don't move. Hold it, Jim. Hold it. Don't move.'

I said 'What's the matter?' He said 'Don't move.' And he comes and takes the cobra out of my hands and he said 'Oh my God, didn't you see? The tape came off.' I said 'The tape came off? Why didn't you say stop?' He said 'Because they said "Action".' Apparently the film was more important than my life! That was the way it was in the old Hollywood days.

You can understand why I wasn't mad about filming. I don't

really think it's a self-respecting job for a man over thirty. But in those days and those films, men were big tall fellers – a different breed from today. I put my foot in it a while back. A reporter came over to interview me. I said 'You don't want to interview me. I've got nothing new to talk about.' He said 'You had a lung out?' I said 'Everbody knows that.' He said 'No they don't.' I said 'Oh well, I'll tell you about that.' So I told him this incredible story about how they thought I had cancer and I had only three months to live and all that and in the end they were wrong.

I had some friends with me as well as the reporter and we were having a few drinks. Then I think the interview's over. And the reporter casually asked what I thought was the difference between Hollywood men of the 40s and those of the 80s.

I said 'When I came to Hollywood in '49 there was Errol Flynn, Tyrone Power, Clark Gable, Gary Cooper, John Wayne, and Cary Grant. Now you've got the five midgets.' (I said it as a joke – not to be published!) 'You've got Dudley Moore, Richard Dreyfuss and so on.' I also said some of the new men are very hairy. Because in those early days, Errol Flynn and Tyrone Power never had any hair. None of us had body hair. Now you get Burt Reynolds, Tom Sellick, and they're hairy aren't they? So I said they're small and hairy. And it was a joke.

But he went and printed it. The next thing there is a headline in a London paper, 'Stewart Granger – Three Months To Live'. Right? The story goes on and tells the whole story including all the joking about the actors that I thought was off the record.

In New York they pick it up too. But the headline there is not 'Granger Three Months To Live'. It's 'Granger takes on Richard Dreyfuss, Dustin Hoffman . . .' They are, let me say immediately, wonderful successful actors!

I had a battle for years, you know, with Hedda Hopper, the gossip columnist. It all began at a party. I was ordered by MGM to take Elizabeth Taylor, who was then sixteen, a gorgeous sixteen, to a party. At the party, there was the horseface with the hat – Hedda Hopper. This was the period when I was married to Jean Simmons, and Michael Wilding was going to be married to Elizabeth Taylor, and they were staying with us.

Hedda Hopper gave orders for Liz and Mike to be interviewed – they didn't ask you, they just used to say 'You will report to Hedda

Hopper at four o'clock.' So Liz and Michael both reported at four o'clock. About five thirty, Mike came back to me, ashen-faced, and said 'Jim, you know what she said? I'm sitting down and she takes Liz away in a corner and says "You can't marry Mike. He's a homosexual".' He says 'Jim, what can you do?' I said 'She said you were homosexual?' I picked up the phone to Hedda Hopper. I said 'Listen, you, how dare you . . .?' Boom!

Time goes by, Liz and Mike make up to Hedda. I never do. So Hedda gives it to me for years. That was 1951.

In 1962 Mike Wilding's on the phone. 'Jim, have you read *Under Your Hat?*, the book by Hedda Hopper!' I said 'I don't read Hedda Hopper. Why?' He said 'She says "I said to Elizabeth Taylor, 'You mustn't marry Michael Wilding because he's a homosexual with Stewart Granger'."'

I started laughing. Then I thought a minute. My mother, who ran a bridge club in Bournemouth, is going to read that. Her friends are going to say 'Is your son gay?' Now I'd been married three times, and I'd got kids!

I said 'What have you done?' He said 'I sued her.' He got $150,000 – like a million and a half today. So I sued her for three million. That's like thirty million today. That was 1962.

In 1972, I'm back in America making a film. I hurt my back and I go to an osteopath. He's doing my back and he said 'You knew Hedda Hopper, didn't you?' My back goes into a spasm. He says 'Oh, her back used to go exactly the same when I talked about you.'

I said 'You talked to Hedda Hopper about me?' He said 'Yes. Would it please you to know that she died in terror of you?' 'Hedda Hopper died in terror of me?' 'Yes. She said "He's going to get every penny I've got. I know him. He beat Howard Hughes."'

I said 'Did she suffer?' He said 'Yes.' I said 'Good!'.

Sophia Loren

SOPHIA LOREN had one of the longest rounds of applause of anyone who has come on 'Wogan'. We have always had mutual respect for each other's body. She loves my knees, suspects that my feet are an erogenous zone, and she even thinks I'm slim. We conversed at a suitably safe distance – first of all about her ideal man.

SOPHIA LOREN: I've worked with many partners, and an ideal man would be a man with the eyes of Paul Newman, the nose of Gregory Peck, the smile of Marlon Brando, the voice of Richard Burton, and the nice, wonderful, slim figure of Mr. Wogan.

WOGAN: There'll be no holding me from now on! For thirty years you've been regarded as one of the most beautiful women in the world.

SOPHIA: Twenty-five years, I think.

WOGAN: OK, twenty-five then. And probably for the next twenty-five you will be so regarded. It must have made you a little vain, a little proud of yourself?

SOPHIA: Well, the word vanity has got a very negative side to it. It's always used about a person who is a very pompous person with nothing inside. But if you think about it, the word vain can also have a positive meaning. After all, what does vain mean? The desire to be right. And there is nothing wrong with that. So, yes, I am vain. And you are too.

I was not always considered beautiful. I used to be called *stuzzicadente*, which means toothpick. But that was a long, long time ago. But as far as looks are concerned, it's what's inside that counts. Appearances are very important. But most of all, it's what you bring from inside of yourself, like kindness, and manners. A beautiful woman can walk in a room, and if she had nothing inside, she would be easily forgotten. Instead, a woman who has a kind of charm and is intelligent, has very nice conversation, even if she is not so beautiful – she is going to catch the eye of every man in the room.

WOGAN: Chaplin said of you that you were a girl raised between a gun factory and an erupting volcano. In other words you have a fiery temperament. Is that true?

SOPHIA: I have quite a fiery temperament, but I don't show it so much. Because I am an actress, I'm always surrounded by many people, and I can't let myself go as much as I would like to sometimes. I try to build up a second nature, so I always look very calm and very tranquil and very disciplined. And when I get home – I break everything!

I don't like to go to parties. I don't like to go out at night. And for these kind of people who like this kind of things, I might be quite boring. I like to be at home and I like to play cards, I look at the television, I like to play Scrabble, I like to play all sorts of games. They relax me. I'm serious! And I don't ever get bored. I put being a mother and a wife before my career. I think being a mother is the most important thing in the world for a woman.

Bob Hope

BOB HOPE is one of the greatest international stars in the world – and so unassuming. When I met him, he was in London organising a charity concert. He spends most of his time either playing golf or lunching with the President of the United States. I was pleased and honoured that he came to Shepherd's Bush Green for an all-too-brief visit – and on his 82nd birthday. Naturally we did not forget a cake: a golf course with 82 candles. Bob looks nothing like his age – and he certainly doesn't act it . . .

WOGAN: How do you keep so spry, so youthful?

BOB HOPE: Same as you, I play golf. Rob people.

WOGAN: You were born in London. Why did you leave so young? It wasn't your decision, obviously.

HOPE: Well, I left when I was four because I realised there was very little chance of me becoming King. I knew I could go to Denmark and be Queen, but I just didn't think . . . I'm glad to be here every once in a while. I have a lot of relatives.

WOGAN: And you're always roving the globe. You never sit still. They tell me *you own* San Fernando Valley. Do you never sit in the old valley and look at it all?

HOPE: No. That's not true. I own half of it.

WOGAN: Do you find you still have much energy to jet around?

HOPE: I was in Ottowa Saturday night, finished the show, flew into Kennedy and flew back here. I fly everywhere. It doesn't bother me. I always carry tranquillisers. But some of the stewardesses won't take them.

WOGAN: How do you get over the jet lag?

HOPE: I don't even pay attention to it. What can you do? You got an eight-hour difference between my place and here. You just have to contend with it.

WOGAN: That's what you call California, isn't it? Your place.

HOPE: Yes. Thank you. I hope the tax people aren't listening.

WOGAN: They never watch this kind of rubbish. Did I see somewhere that you were once a pugilist?

HOPE: Yes, I don't mention that much. I fought under the name of Packy Easts. After my second fight, the manager wanted to change it to Mae West's. I would have won my last fight, but the referee stepped on my hand.

WOGAN: You've entertained almost every President, from Roosevelt to Reagan. Indeed you've played golf many a time over here with Gerry Ford. How come you're so well in with the various Presidents?

HOPE: I don't know. We're invited, you know, to do the White House dinners and things like that. You meet them, and they invite you to the White House. You get a free meal. A little bit of government money back. Ford is my favourite. I have a special caddy when I play with him. He's the same blood type as I am. And he's made golf a contact sport.

WOGAN: You're a man of enormous stature in America – and you're pretty tall here! How come you never went for political office yourself?

HOPE: The money wasn't right. No, in fact on Thursday night I'm going to be with President Reagan at the Washington Convention Centre. Since he's been President a lot of people in show business are thinking about going in. They asked me to, but I told them 'The money's not right, and anyway my wife wouldn't want

24

to move to a smaller house.' I think Reagan would like to be royalty. In fact, I know he's hoping for a promotion. But a lot of people are thinking of running for that office. Like Charlton Heston . . . He played Moses you know, and led the people out of Egypt. So Reagan will probably make him a director of transportation.

WOGAN: What about the movies? What were the ones you had most fun making?

HOPE: I think the *On the Road* pictures we had most fun. Because Bing Crosby and I were just wild, trying to top each other. It was sensational. Seven weeks of that, I mean, was just too much. But I enjoyed making all the movies.

WOGAN: How long since you made your last movie?

HOPE: About twelve years.

WOGAN: Is there any possibility that you're ever going to retire?

HOPE: I don't know – how do you spell that?

Paul McCartney

W HO WOULD ever guess that Paul McCartney has grown-up kids and is in his mid-forties? But then, he probably says the same thing about me . . . However, one of us has aged better than the other; I think he has taken ageing lessons from Cliff Richard. I've heard they share an attic, and every so often go up there to admire each other's paintings . . .

McCartney is puckish and entirely likeable, with not a jot of pomposity nor affectation to him. I'm not very good on idols and I haven't been a fan of anybody since Gene Autry in about 1948, but if ever Paul McCartney took to the saddle with a white hat, gloves and a guitar, I'm not sure that I could control myself . . .

The motivation to write a good song is the same now as it ever was. Originally, not having any money, we used to write a song and say 'Well, there's a swimming pool'. But the real motivation was just that we enjoyed doing it. And it's still the same. I still want to make a decent record. I just actually enjoy making records. A lot of people ask me if I should jack it in or something. But I just actually enjoy doing it. I think I'd do it for a hobby if I didn't do it for a profession.

I always try to apply a sort of critical assessment to myself, but sometimes a little dross slips through. I think in the end you've got to like the song yourself. It's the same with remembering them too. When John Lennon and I started, we'd write a song on the Tuesday, and we didn't have tape recorders in those days, so if we'd forgotten it on the Wednesday, it was clearly not a good song.

I obviously miss John and miss having him around. We had bad times, like anyone. But he was such a major talent and such a great feller. I think everyone misses him, not just me. But I miss him particularly on the songwriting. I'd have a hard time finding anyone that good.

I have always kept busy – that's why after the Beatles split up I thought 'if I don't form a band and I don't keep in the business, then after a couple of years I'm going to find I can't sing'. And I haven't got that kind of knack in front of an audience. You can lose it dead easy. As you've noticed! So I did it really just to sort of keep oiled like an athlete – to keep going in case I ever wanted to get serious again.

I like the kick that other people give you. The only time I ever really got out on my own was when we did Live Aid. And then my mike went off! That was terrifying. In front of fifty billion people. But I wouldn't give music up for the world.

I am not coping with getting old very well, but in truth, I don't really mind too much. Because it's a whole different thing that's happening to you. When I was twenty it was screaming fans and all that, which was great for a bachelor. Now I'm 44 – and I'm a Dad with teenage children.

I remember – in fact, it's one of my earliest memories – being about five years old, and thinking, 'I might well be a Dad'. And it was a very weird thing, to actually think you'd be telling people what to do in life. But that is what I like about middle age. It's different altogether. You're learning new stuff every day. It's not your bachelor days at all.

I feel sorry for the kids, being in the spotlight all the time. But I'm very lucky, my kids are pretty normal. I've seen friends of mine who've gone the other route, and they've given their kids the nannies, and flash cars, stuff like that. And it spoils them. Kids get so they don't appreciate anything. So at the risk of being called a skinflint, I've always tried to treat mine about how I was treated. Perhaps a little better because obviously I've got a bit more money than my Dad had – and a few better ideas. He had a great explanation for the facts of life. He said 'See those Alsatians over there?' And that was it!

27

The kids have resented me occasionally, like any kids would. They say 'But I want five sweaters.' You say 'Shut up, you're having one . . . if you're lucky.' But I tell you, they do appreciate that one sweater more. We're a pretty close family, and we can talk things out. My oldest daughter Heather is 23 now. And she was into punk a lot. They were good kids, but they looked aggressive on the surface. But her friends were very nice. We did have a couple of arguments, obviously when they're teenage. She stormed off once, she went to see her friends. But she was nice, she came back and explained to me what had happened. She said to her friends that she'd had an argument with the old man, and her friends turned round and said 'Don't worry, any trouble from him and you can go to the newspapers.' So I thought it was time to move house.

As far as the kids go, I had some unfortunate publicity a few years ago about taking cannabis. I ended up in jail in Japan. On the one hand you want to say to the kids 'Stay clean, don't do anything. Stay healthy and enjoy your life'. Which I think is the number one aim. I do advise them to do that. But it was a bit hypocritical when I was in clink somewhere. In actual fact, I explained to them how I see the whole thing, and what I think is very dangerous, and obviously warn them like mad about stuff like heroin and very serious stuff. My Dad would take a drink, and stuff like that. So you can't say do nothing. They're maybe going to do something. So I just try and minimise the risk by telling them.

But let's face it, you start that kind of thing to have fun. It's like alcohol. You start it for a bit of a buzz. But once it starts to take hold on you, it's not fun any more. So anyone who's been through that kind of addiction I feel sorry for.

Jeffrey Archer and Lord Soper

J EFFREY ARCHER was Britain's youngest MP when his failure in a business venture forced him to resign from the House of Commons. He then became one of the world's top-selling authors. He returned to the political arena (which was something he had longed for) when Mrs. Thatcher appointed him deputy chairman of the Conservative party, only to resign after the affair of the call girl and the £2,000.

Lord Soper on the other hand has for 60 years been one of this country's most visible Christians and probably its most vocal, preaching as he does not only from the pulpit but on Tower Hill and at Speaker's Corner in Hyde Park.

Before Jeffrey Archer's case was heard in court (a case which he of course won), they both met on 'Wogan' for a surprising conversation. Jeffrey was brave enough to talk but seemed, not surprisingly, a little nervous.

WOGAN: Can I ask you, as a person who knows you from television, and as an observer, how could you have got yourself into such a mess?

JEFFREY ARCHER: We all make mistakes in life. I seem to do mine publicly.

WOGAN: You have the nerve to admit it anyway. How did your family react?

ARCHER: Mary, my wife, was tremendous. And the children didn't really understand what was going on. I think in public life people don't realise the strain children go through, whether you're a success or a failure or whatever happens. I thought it was a great

29

credit to their mother and the way she's brought them up that they were tremendously resilient.

WOGAN: What about Mrs. Thatcher – what was her reaction?

ARCHER: She's tremendous. She has a public image where everybody sees her as a sort of tough, hard woman running Great Britain Ltd., which is the way she has to be if you run Great Britain Ltd. Then when something personal happens, she's immensely sympathetic and caring. It's a side that anyone who's been in any form of trouble knows about her. In many ways it's sad that the public can't see that side because it's not part of her public life.

WOGAN: What has been the public reaction?

ARCHER: You're the first person to talk about it, Terry. Everyone else has been very kind and not bothered. I'm bound to say, if people stand by you, and you see how many good friends you've got, it goes a lot quicker than you had feared. I had over 1,700 letters from people all over the country, many from socialists, saying that they were appalled by the way I was treated. Many would basically always vote socialist, and didn't agree with my philosophy, but felt it wasn't the way to treat someone.

WOGAN: Has your nasty experience taught you humility?

ARCHER: I think if you go through anything like this it not only teaches you humility, it frightens the blooming life out of you. It makes you realise who your friends are. And it makes you realise who are good people and strong people and reliable people.

WOGAN: It might be seen as slightly naive?

ARCHER: Yes, certainly. But is this a failing? So someone has to get up and say 'No, I'm never naive. I'm cynical about everything. I never make a mistake.' Yes, I do make mistakes, but I refuse to be cynical. And if into the bargain I'm naive because of that, so be it.

WOGAN: Lord Soper, your thoughts – do you admire naivety?

LORD S: I admire innocence. But naivety is the absence of intelligence. Naive people are those who haven't thought carefully.

WOGAN: Somebody said the other day that you cannot be a Christian and not vote Tory.

LORD S: Well, that's obviously a decayed mental process. I think it's more difficult for Tories to get to heaven but I think they'll get there by circuitous routes.

ARCHER: We shall privatise heaven before you get there!

LORD S: What we need today is a new conception of what politics is all about. It isn't privatisation. Politics is community. And we've got a country at the moment divided in two, north and south. I want that unity to be re-established. But it can only come when you're prepared to give other people the benefit of the doubt.

ARCHER: I do think the north versus south – which I accept – is a problem. I don't deny that. It's not helped by men of your position continually referring to it. I don't know how often you go up there. I was up there last week – I was in Pontefract, Dewsbury, and Bradford. I found a lot of northern people are fairly insulted by the suggestion that southerners are continually feeling sorry for them.

LORD S: I don't feel sorry for them. I do feel that there is an increasing gap between the two communities. That gap militates against any sense that we belong to each other. Socialism is not nationalisation, it isn't everybody owning everything. Socialism is the recognition that we sit at the same table and we're entitled to the same amount of food according to our needs. We belong to one another. We cannot have a society today if individual preference is regarded as absolute. It's the caring for one another and the brotherhood.

ARCHER: It's very hard for anyone who believes in capitalism the way I do to become a socialist. I will never be a socialist. And it's very hard for someone like you, Lord Soper, to join us. But maybe you've still got time. I'll give you another 20 years.

Donald and I don't agree politically on many things, but I do think that one of the most exciting things that's happened in politics in the world today is Gorbachev. We have a world leader on the stage today who is obviously highly intelligent, sophisti-

31

cated, and is going to be there until the turn of the century. Therefore it's very important to Europe and to America. We've got a man now in the Soviet Union who's making revolutionary changes by the standards we understood ten or fifteen years ago, or even as little as five years ago. We've got to give him a chance.

There is this attitude among cynical politicians that all Russians are evil and they would kill us at the first opportunity. That's fine. You obviously keep that in the forefront of your mind. But I think Gorbachev would like to see, by the turn of the century, a totally different Russia from the one he was brought up in. I believe he genuinely would like to see an economic revolution in that country and bring the standard of living inside Russia much higher within his lifetime. I'd like to see the Western world give him the opportunity to prove it.

I've always hoped that if he came out of Afghanistan, that would be such a brave gesture for a new Russian leader. Then Reagan would have to react. He'd have to do something positive himself. I do dislike this business whenever they meet that they have to make a rude statement about each other just after they've parted. I wish we could put that on one side, even if it were just for a year, to give both sides the benefit of the doubt. Because at the end what really matters is the peace and freedom of the world.

LORD S: Could you come over on to our side?

WOGAN: No, he can't.

ARCHER: It's absolute bunkum that socialists always think the morals are on their side. We've just as much morals and good on our side. And we're just as proud of it, sir.

LORD S: I wasn't questioning your morality. I was congratulating you on it. I don't mind privatisation on principle. What I do applaud is this realisation, which I'm so happy to hear you talk about, that what we need today is to put bygones as bygones, and not assume that you first of all categorise the Russians as evil, and Reagan as good, and start off from there. It's utterly wrong. We're all a bunch of sinners, even you and I.

WOGAN: Would you like me to come in with a question?

ARCHER: Oh, I thought you'd gone home!

Vicky Clement-Jones

V ICKY CLEMENT-JONES was a remarkable lady. Five
years ago, she was a senior registrar at Bart's Hospital.
Amongst her responsibilities was that of counselling patients
who had developed cancer. Then, sadly, she herself was
diagnosed as having advanced ovarian cancer. She was told
her condition was inoperable and she would only have three
months to live. That was 1982. In early 1987 she was still going
strong, thanks to amazing willpower coupled with painful
treatment. During her illness, she found the time and energy
to set up an organisation to help other cancer patients and
their relatives deal with all traumas associated with cancer.

Before the diagnosis, I was taken into hospital. When I was coming
round from an anaesthetic, a young house doctor came to see me.
He had such a look on his face, I thought there must be something
seriously wrong. But he could not tell me. He said, 'The professor
will come and see you tomorrow.' I thought, 'I'm still dreaming.'
But the next morning the professor did come, and the reality was
that I did have advanced cancer.

As a doctor myself, I thought I'd only got three months to live. I
honestly didn't think there was much hope. I went through all the
feelings of shock, devastation – my whole world suddenly came to
a grinding halt. I felt angry. 'Why me?' I thought. 'It happens to
other people, but not to me.'

I'd been a practising doctor for ten years. And although I'd
looked after cancer patients in those ten years, I came to realise as I
crossed that divide from doctor to patient that I really had no idea
of what it was like to have cancer, and that I hadn't really been

offering very much to cancer patients before.

I remember the surgeons looking after me, the people who did the original biopsy. They were very gloomy about my outlook. They had problems talking about cancer with me.

Thinking back to the time when I was a doctor, I can think of many patients where I really feel we failed them. You go on a ward round and somebody is ill with cancer. You think you are unlikely to give them curative treatment, and you try to avoid them. You don't look at them. You sort of hurry quickly by. And really, there are things we *can* do to improve the quality of life, however long or short they have.

My husband did the very difficult job, when I was first diagnosed, of ringing round and telling family and friends. At a time when he was feeling low and with not much hope, he had to try and instil some hope in them. Some of our friends have completely disappeared since. I'm not saying they were good friends, but people who were at university with us. We might have had dinner with them once or twice a year. He told them I had cancer, and they've never contacted us since. I find it extraordinary.

There are still myths about cancer. Some people do think cancer is infectious. I remember a cancer patient telling me that she would go out into the garden and if a neighbour was there – one with whom she used to chat over the wall – the neighbour would go running in. There are other bizarre things like somebody said to a cancer patient, 'I don't know why you've got cancer. You were always so clean.' And other very odd things. I think healthy people also feel guilty that they're not ill with cancer themselves, and they don't know what to say. They're maybe frightened that you'll talk about your illness, or talk about death. Which is another taboo.

So, in some ways it's the cancer patient that has to reach out to people by making it easier for *them*. That's what I did for my friends, because I really needed them. I'd been in hospital for weeks and weeks, and my husband too would need my support. I used to get my friends to come round and bake me cakes. They would take me round with them in a wheelchair, and give me things to do and show other people you're still a normal person, even though you're ill with cancer.

So, to help other people in my position, I have set up an organisation called 'Bacup' – the British Association of Cancer

34

United Patients and their families and friends. A lot of the problems people have is to do with the relationship with doctors. They don't understand the medical terms being used. They're frightened of the treatment or investigations. So we provide medical information to help people understand what they are about to go through and to help them make decisions about their treatment. Since we launched the information service, we've handled twenty thousand enquiries. It's a remarkable number.

We hope we provide practical information to cope with practical problems. I went through fourteen months of intensive treatment and during that time I had to learn to cope from square one. Like, when I was having chemotherapy, losing my hair. The doctors told me I would lose my hair and they issued an NHS wig. But what they didn't tell me was of the several weeks when the hair was actually falling out and what it would be like. I'd wake up every morning with hair all over the bed, in my mouth and eyes, and it'd take me an hour to pluck the hair from my bedclothes. At the end of this, there was hair all over the bed again. There was another time when I was out with my mother trying to be as normal as possible. We were in an Italian restaurant and I was drinking minestrone soup. I looked down and there were clumps of hair which had fallen down. This really upset me. I said to myself, 'Vicky, there must be an answer'. I racked my brains for several days, and I finally came up with a solution, and sent my mother out to buy a hair net. I wore the hair net in bed at night, and in the morning I just shook it out. Unless you've been through it, you don't think about it.

People ask me about the quality of life. Well, the quality matches the expectations. I can eat but I can't eat normally because of having had too many operations on the bowel. I get quality of life by not asking for too much. Instead of railing against the fact that I can't go out and have grand dinners any more, or run the marathon, I concentrate on the things I can do. Like enjoying my garden or going out with friends.

This intelligent, admirable and very brave lady died not long after this interview, in August. It was a privilege to meet her, and help to publicise what she was trying to do. May the work she started continue and prosper; it would be a fitting tribute.

Boy George

I FIRST interviewed Boy George at the very peak of his success, a couple of years ago. Then, it seemed as if the whole world was bowing and scraping before him. Boy George imitators sprang up on every side.

Just as quickly, the fad was over. The hits no longer came; the vultures of the tabloids hovered over George's every move, and he gave them plenty to write about . . .

It has been a very bad year for me with the drugs, the trial and the publicity, but everything is now behind me. Hopefully it'll go away in time. I think if I'm going to apologise to anybody it wouldn't be Fleet Street. It would be the kids really and the people who have supported me. I've had a lot of love, which is something that really helps you get over any problem. I've always had hate mail, regardless of my problems. But people have been very, very supportive, and have understood. Which has been very good. I did expect people to say 'It serves you right'. Fair comment in a way. But people have been wonderful, really good.

I think a lot of young adults round about my age go through a self-destructive period. It was a lot to do with success and not being able to handle it, not really understanding it; wondering where I was a lot of the time and just running away from reality. That's what it's all about. Perhaps everything happened too soon for me. You feel strange when you sort of come from nothing, and all these things happen. And this industry is full of people who want to get you high, or mess you up. A lot of the time the only way to do it is with drugs. I have just been stupid and silly.

I'm very lucky, you know, because I've got a great job. That's the thing that brought me back to my senses. Just to look around – I've done wonderful things, I've had a great time. And the affection that I've had. You think, well, so many people care, you have to be responsible. You have to care back, show emotion.

I lost a very important friend, and I think that was a real bang on the head for me. That was why I went for treatment. It's sad that it takes something like that, but it really did affect me. A lot of people around me are still very ill. I still see people who are having problems. I don't scorn them. I just think it's very sad. It's very tragic. The problem with the media is they don't really understand what the problem is. They just see it as something very sensational.

I know my brother told everyone of the full extent of my drug addiction, but he did it out of affection. He's my brother and I love him. I've no malice against him at all. In a way it was a shock. He didn't get paid for it. Both my parents have been brilliant. My father especially, who has been very ill. He's been very strong, which has really impressed me. I didn't expect him to hold up through it and I felt very guilty about that. It was 'What am I doing to them?' especially when I saw all the things in the papers about my family. They were being run down and everything – 'the dotty O'Dowds'.

The main thing I think with things like drugs, is that you upset people who really love you, especially your family. My advice to young people is that it really isn't worth it. It isn't a good idea – and I mean *any* kind of drugs.

A lot of people are addicted to alcohol, or cigarettes. I think if you are that kind of person then that's where the problem starts. If you jump in the deep end, you're going to have a real problem. Things like heroin destroy your body. My doctor told me it's going to take me a long, long time before I feel perfectly normal again. I thought it would be over in about two weeks. So I'm paying the price now. I'm taking it very, very calmly. But I think you have to occupy yourself. There are so many leeches out there who want to drag you back down. So you have to be very strong . . .

I want to make records. I want to make people happy. For a long time I've made people miserable. I think people are really tired of seeing a haggard-looking Boy George.

Liv Ullman

L IV ULLMAN turned out to be a completely different
person from all those morose and serious parts that she
plays. Why should it be that such a beautiful lady deals in such
gloom and doom. Well, she *is* Norwegian and they have had a
bad press in the rest of Europe. Maybe it's something to do
with their ancestors going berserk and raping and pillaging in
those silly hats. I think those movies with her husband,
Ingmar Bergman, have a lot to do with it too.

All producers and directors, they see my face and they say
'Anguish'. That happened in Norway for years and years. I met
Ingmar and he said 'Anguish'. And he fell in love, and so it went
on. I don't know why we Norwegians have a reputation as an
anguished people. We have no reason to be. We don't rape any
more. I don't rape. But when you meet a director like Ingmar
Bergman, he doesn't exactly write comedies, although I think I
could be wonderful in comedies. But living with him, working with
him, that's not living with Bob Hope, you know. Not many gags.
Other people at breakfast will sit and have coffee and little sweet
rolls and maybe say wonderful things to each other. When I lived
with Ingmar Bergman, when we met for breakfast or something,
he told me his nightmares, and I knew I had to star in them.

Directors see me as gloomy. They tend to stick me in a lot of
frumpy old clothes. I always played plays by authors who were
dead. I have never in my life been on the stage, really, or showed
my legs even. I have okay legs, too. When I did a musical (it was

called *I Remember Mama*), now, I thought, I'm going to be glamorous and wonderful – and all they fitted me for was an apron! That was my costume. When Lauren Bacall gets to do a musical, she has feather boas and everything. They gave *me* a mop and a bucket!

I can't really sing. But I had seven songs. My first song was called 'Stuffed Cabbage'. That's not so glamorous. And they say in a musical you must never have children with you, or animals. When I was singing and doing my things I was with five children and two cats. Dancing in front of me.

My dream is to do a play for a writer who is still alive. And I'm going to do it – a play by Harold Pinter. Now I have my legs all over the stage. But while I am flinging my legs all over the stage, Nicola Pagett is sitting there and I think she is one of the most beautiful women I've ever met. I can't win.

But apart from acting, much of my time is taken up now with working for UNICEF around the world. The children I have met are cheerful. They are trusting. They are lovely. Let me tell you just one little story.

People think that caring and tending for children far away, that's sad and it's too much of an effort, so they tend not to do it. I remember especially one little girl in India, and she was just brought in from the streets. She had been an orphan all her life, living on the street. And she was sitting there on a bed for the first time in her life. Although we didn't share a language, we were 'talking' – talking the way you do. She was stroking my hair, and I saw she had a little ring on her finger, a beautiful ring with a red glass dome. I wanted to show her that I thought it was lovely. So I stroked it. And she just took it off and she gave it to me. It is the ring I am wearing now.

Why I'm telling the story is that we never know when we give something, even very little, what will happen. This little ring, wherever it has been, people have sent in money. People have done fund-raising in the name of this ring. Today I think this ring has collected maybe 100,000 dollars.

I may have had my preconceptions about Liv Ullman – but she certainly had her own about me. She automatically assumed that as a Celt I would have worn a skirt!

Bob Geldof

HERE'S A little quiz. Who do you know who's been a pea processor, a navvy on the M25, a squatter, an assistant in an abattoir, an English teacher, a mousecatcher, a hot dog salesman, an actor, a writer, and described by no less an authority than Prince William as 'all dirty, with scruffy hair and wet shoes'. I met Bob Geldof after the famous Live Aid concert – watched by 50 billion people – and just before he expected the whole planet to run in the 'Race against Time'. I began by asking him if he had ever stopped to think why it was *he* who was chosen to organise such intensive famine relief:

Chosen is too strong a word. There were lots of factors. Because the band weren't doing great at the time, so maybe it meant I had time. Sting saw the same horrifying pictures on the TV news and felt the same reactions, but he was going off to do things, touring and so on – and I think so many events and time conspired to make it more easy for *me* to do it than perhaps other people. Sometimes in the middle of Live Aid I'd lie awake – I can distance myself quite easily and see what's going on – but it seemed that events were happening outside of myself. At points like that you sort of think 'What the hell's going on here?'

There was a thing in *Life* magazine at Christmas where they asked 'Why him?' and they supposed that some fallible God had come down from heaven to find somebody who would go on and do Live Aid and knocked at the wrong door. That was their attitude. It's not that glamorous a thing, it's not that glorious. It's something I wanted to do and that I thought would make £72,000. But events got bigger and bigger and I just stayed with it. Mainly I stayed with it because I said every penny would get there, and I wanted to live up to that. Every penny turned out to be over a hundred million dollars, so I'm still there.

I think the interesting thing is that things like Food Aid and Comic Relief and all that are still going long after the pictures have gone off our screens. This means that people not only care but they care for long periods of time. I thought maybe we were crisis orientated, that as soon as the pictures went away everyone would forget. The fact that everyone remembers must, I think, frighten a lot of politicians. The main reason for Sport Aid is not so much the money, though that's crucial and critical still, but on the day after the Race Against Time is the UN General Assembly debate for the *first time ever* on the crisis on the continent of Africa.

If everyone participates, they will come out of that building possibly for the first time in their bloody lives having actually achieved something! They will be listening – they *have* to listen – to quite literally the planet doing something again and demanding some sort of coherent action from a bunch of people we usually expect incoherency from. Believe me, just the pressure that that puts on the creeps who will be meeting from all over the world will be enough to finally make them do something. People do care. These people in Africa are not going to be allowed to die in misery.

And I am pleased to say that the Food Aid book, compiled by Delia Smith with recipes from 'Wogan' guests and viewers, made £1 million for famine relief.

HRH
the Princess Royal

PRINCESS ANNE, or as she is now The Princess Royal, was the first member of the Royal Family to brave the Television Theatre and 'Wogan' – and a delightful guest she was too. Subsequently, she braved Emlyn Hughes on 'A Question of Sport'. The woman knows no fear!

At the time Princess Anne could not do anything right – if you believed the press. There were rumours that she was not getting on with the Princess of Wales, that her dress sense was not all that it should be, and that she was a lousy jockey. But her performance on the show revealed her to the British public as the intelligent, witty, and compassionate person that she is. Her appearance on 'Wogan' transformed the Royal image. As an old hand at royal engagements, I asked her how she learned and if she passed on advice.

WOGAN: Do you find the various engagements you take on an enormous strain? You must do. Who offers advice on how to cope with these appearances, what to do, what to say? Have you generally learnt from experience yourself? I know you write all your own speeches.

PRINCESS ANNE: You learn the hard way, mostly. And experience.

WOGAN: Do you give any advice to, say, the Princess of Wales on how to deal with engagements?

PRINCESS ANNE: I couldn't really call it advice. You can only repeat, I think, your own experiences and the problems that you've had and the way you've countered them or got over them. It's important to remember what it was like when you first started. How you struggled to think of things to say, and what sort of line you were going to take, the sort of questions you were likely to ask, and how people react. But that really only does come with experience. You can only help – if it helps – by telling how you found it. And of course each individual reacts completely differently.

WOGAN: The thing that always strikes me as a formidable task is the endless reviewing lines at, say, a premiere or a BAFTA award. How can you think of something new to say to each one you come up to? Apart from 'I loved the movie'?

PRINCESS ANNE: Well, they usually introduce you before you see the movie. Or you're opening something you haven't seen, which happens quite a lot. I'm very short about it. I say I'm very much looking forward to seeing whatever it is I'm about to open. Or words to that effect. But I frequently thank them for having the opportunity of seeing it before opening if I'm allowed to! It depends. You can play it two ways. You can ask everybody – rather like a sort of market research – literally everybody, the same questions. So you have three questions for that afternoon and you ask everybody the same questions. And with any luck it shortens the time involved, because if the person standing next to the one you're talking to is paying any attention he'll have the answers ready for you. It doesn't always happen!

WOGAN: There have been tales in the press of you and the Princess of Wales not exactly hitting it off?

PRINCESS ANNE: Yes. One of their better fairy stories. Usually it's not worth saying anything in reply. The fact that it was just a story in the first place means they'll take anything you say and it will come out on their side.

WOGAN: You've missed a couple of Royal occasions – you missed the Queen's coronation, didn't you? They wouldn't let you go to that!

PRINCESS ANNE: True. They wouldn't let me go. I was sort of

43

tied to the rocking horse all morning. I don't think I knew what was going on but I was annoyed about being left behind, irrespective of what it was I was being left behind from!

WOGAN: And then they wrenched you from your tutors, and sent you off to Benenden.

PRINCESS ANNE: I'm afraid they didn't wrench me. I volunteered. With tutors, there's really only you and them. And that requires an awful lot of concentration. There are certain advantages to being lost in a class!

WOGAN: How did they treat you? Was there any bullying?

PRINCESS ANNE: I wasn't that big a girl! No, I don't think so. I wasn't really aware of any. But I didn't set out to. I'm very quiet. I kept my eyes and ears open.

WOGAN: When you finished at Benenden, it is said you could have gone on to University. But unlike your brothers you didn't choose to do so.

PRINCESS ANNE: Well, I must admit that at the time I was rather influenced by the fact that I thought there were quite a lot of my contemporaries who were going to university simply because it was university. They didn't seem to be going for any particular reason. Just experience. At that stage, I was being included by the Queen on some of her visits, and I rather hoped to go abroad with her as well. So I just felt that that was possibly more constructive from my point of view and more interesting than it would have been going to university.

A lot of people think that on any Royal visit you don't see anything, that you only meet grand people and you only see what they want to show you. And of course that rather assumes that you never look out of the window and are stone deaf as well, and incapable of asking questions! I learnt a lot, I think. We went to some very interesting places.

There's this wonderful phrase, ordinary people. They may have been the top people in the country, but equally there must have been a very good reason for them having got there in the first place. It was a view, certainly, and you could legitimately be criticised for it being one kind of view, but nonetheless they were worth talking to and asking questions.

WOGAN: When you see your elder brother, and indeed your younger brother, taking part in university reviews and madcap gaiety like that, don't you miss that?

PRINCESS ANNE: I did that in the Girl Guides!

WOGAN: Now you're the Chancellor of the University of London.

PRINCESS ANNE: Strange, isn't it? They were given the choice, that's all I can say. But don't you think it's a very good idea for a University Chancellor not to have been to university? Don't you think it gives them a much better outlook – than somebody more introverted? Certainly I think it's been of great benefit to me, because I've learnt all sorts of things on my visits to the various colleges.

WOGAN: Are you conscious of the fact that what we call in this business, your image, has improved over the past few years?

PRINCESS ANNE: Are you telling me? I tend to wonder – I like to ask people what they were expecting, before they met me. Then I find out what my image was.

WOGAN: All public figures are security risks. To what extent is your private life hampered by security?

PRINCESS ANNE: Nowadays, not really. Because living in Gloucestershire and on a farm is really quite off the beaten track, and out of the public view, it's not really too difficult. You're at home, and not very much in evidence. In public on your official engagements, of course, it's an occupational hazard. But I think while you're busy and going about talking to people, you don't really notice. That's not to say other people don't notice. It tends to be rather more obvious from the outside than it is from where you are.

WOGAN: Do you and Captain Phillips ever get a chance to go out on your own, say, for a quiet meal?

PRINCESS ANNE: Yes. Because being in a reasonably quiet

rural area, that's not really very difficult. There are actually some decent restaurants down there. I'm not going to tell you where they are!

WOGAN: You're under constant scrutiny as far as your appearance goes. Are you fed up with that?

PRINCESS ANNE: Yes. It's a little bit more entertaining now. Obviously in the past I wasn't sufficiently interested in clothes really to be of interest to anybody. And that again didn't fit the image. So whatever I wore was going to be bad news. And inevitably it takes people a long time to find their feet in terms of what's going to suit them. Certainly for any young person. It's just taken me longer than most, that's all.

WOGAN: Do you still care about clothes, or not?

PRINCESS ANNE: They're more the functional part of the working side of my life. More than anything else. Clothes are for official functions, and you have to think of the sort of things that you do and places you go, and climates you're working in, and what you're going to be doing when you get there. So that limits it somewhat. Also the fact that you'd like them to last marginally longer than six months. So in that sense you can't really follow fashion too much because you simply can't wear them again.

WOGAN: Are you terribly thrifty about your clothes?

PRINCESS ANNE: Terribly.

WOGAN: Are you thrifty about everything?

PRINCESS ANNE: Yes. I think so. Probably. Yes. I had a Scottish nanny.

WOGAN: What would you do if Royalty was abolished?

PRINCESS ANNE: I'd have to work even harder on the farm!

WOGAN: Is there anything you'd really like to do, any career you would have liked to have pursued if you hadn't been the Royal Princess? Would you have qualified as a heavy goods vehicle driver?

PRINCESS ANNE: On the basis that one didn't have a farm to

work on or there was no alternative, both my husband and I have heavy goods vehicle licences, his is an HGV1 and mine is an HGV 3. So in fact it seemed like a very logical way of earning one's living. There is in fact quite a demand for good horsebox drivers. We know one end of a horse from another, you see. We thought we could probably crack that one between us!

WOGAN: You yourself are going to get involved in racing at Epsom in the near future, I hear. On the flat. Do you think, knowing who you are, the other riders, and possibly even horses, are going to withdraw to the rails or get out of your way, or even throw the race?

PRINCESS ANNE: I suppose I could go a very long way round the outside. My trainer might not be too pleased about that.

WOGAN: But you're going to be the automatic favourite.

PRINCESS ANNE: That would be very foolish.

WOGAN: Are you as fit as you would like to be for it? Are you doing weight training, or circuit training? Or Jane Fonda aerobics?

PRINCESS ANNE: I couldn't manage that.

WOGAN: Did you have any bets yourself?

PRINCESS ANNE: No. Gave that up a long time ago. When I was about twelve.

WOGAN: Lost all your pocket money?

PRINCESS ANNE: Yes. To my nanny!

And, as followers of form will acknowledge, the Princess fulfilled her ambitions. She has won three times on the flat and once over the hurdles.

Sean Connery

ONE OF the most pleasurable shows for me was when I was able to combine a few days' golf at the celebrated Turnberry Golf Course in Scotland and, by the wonders of television technology, actually broadcast 'Wogan' from the hotel. It was also a way to pin down Sean Connery who was playing with me in the Pro-Am tournament that week.

By his own admission, Sean does not like to give interviews but he promised me just one if I let him win the next day. Anyway I had always wanted to do my Bond impersonation from *Goldfinger* 'Strict rules of golf, Mr Bond!' In between talk about golf, I was able to learn a little about the bronzed Mr. Connery.

Golf has been one of the greatest things in my life ninety per cent of the time, and ten per cent of the time – well, I would rather not say! I've one regret, that I didn't start golf earlier. I could have lost *all* my hair by the time I was 28! I've always loved sport. In my younger days I played for East Fife. Then I was keen to play for Manchester United, but I was 23, I think, and the average age of their team was 17 or 18 so I was too old. If I had joined them at that time I would have been one of those guys who got it in the Munich disaster.

My road to acting was like this: I was in the Navy for a while but was invalided out – I had ulcers – and was given the chance to become either a tailor, a barber or a French polisher. I chose French polisher because I thought I could, with a motorbike, go

The Great Man, dressed for the hinterland of Shepherd's Bush.

Shortly after this was taken, the inflamed audience turned on Wogan and he had to be carried off with minor contusions.

This boy could have been a male model if he could have kept the weight down.

A little-known fact. Wogan's knees have been bequeathed to the Smithsonian Institute for future generations to wonder at.

Roger Moore — Cubby Broccoli, the producer of the Bond movies, assured me that Roger only got the Bond job because my ears were too big.

HRH The Princess Royal — the first Royal on 'Wogan'.

Simon Weston — a 'Man of the Year' in 1986, and any other year.

A relaxed moment in hostility. Wogan, as you see, has dispensed with his stays.

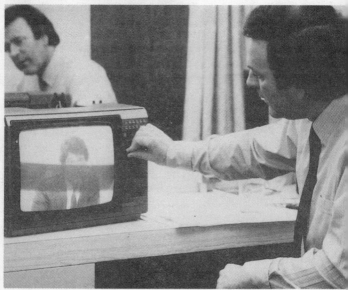

Wogan having trouble with his horizontal hold — a fault that has dogged him throughout his career.

A Christmas gift from me to Sue Ellen — J.R. applauds in anticipation.

First thing every morning, he turns to the cartoon section of the *Financial Times*.

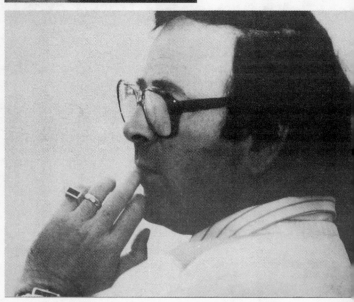

A moment's thought, then on with the show ...

After a wonderful career in films, then folks, just imagine ending up on 'Wogan'.

Sophia Loren — the best knees in the business.

Felix Bowness, warm-up man extraordinaire, whipping the audience up to a frenzy.

Shortly after this picture was taken, Wogan retired to the country with a dozen bottles of Grecian 2000.

Wogan in the dark, as he so often is.

'We are not amused.'

We are not amused.

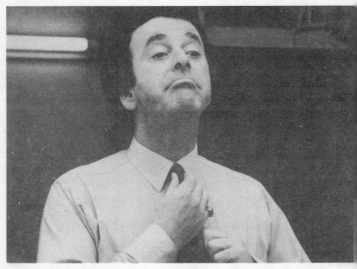

Seconds to take-off, would suicide be the best way out?

All food for use in hospitality has to be tested in advance by the Great Man.

The perfect headgear for going 'beresk' in Shepherd's Bush.

David Attenborough — taking a well-earned rest from interfering in the sex life of spiders.

Vicky Clement-Jones — very brave and sadly missed.

Zsa Zsa Gabor — the well-known Hungarian philosopher.

You should see this boy when he's rested?

out and make a few quid on the side. I ended up polishing coffins!

In my spare time, I did a lot of bodybuilding – you know, pumping iron – and in a way, that is how I got my first acting part. I came south to take part in a 'Mr. Universe' contest at the Scala Theatre. I was much prettier then, of course. While I was there, I heard about the auditions for a show called *South Pacific*. I auditioned, got a part, and went on tour.

It was years later that I landed the Bond part. I wasn't even a Fleming fan. I hadn't read any of the books. When I had been approved for the part, as it were, I was given a couple of them to read. *Dr. No* and *From Russia With Love*, I think. Then I was introduced to Ian Fleming and spent some time with him. He was a very, very interesting man. A terrible snob. A great companion. He knew about everything. I think some of the records he created as an athlete at Eton still stand.

Anyway, what they got was a fairly rough-hewn Edinburgh lad who had to learn about Martinis being shaken and not stirred. But I had the good fortune to work with a man who was a great connoisseur, raconteur and gourmet. You see, I was not that greatly experienced as a film actor, only as a stage actor. He had been in the Guards and we shared the same sense of humour. He taught me a lot about his world and a great deal of the success of the Bond films really should be attributed to him. Eventually the screen character of Bond evolved.

Sean was obviously anxious to go out onto the fairway again, but there was just one question I had to ask him . . . what did he think of his successor as Bond, Roger Moore? The reply was everything I expected from the original 007; after only a moment's pause, he said 'Who?'!

So I thought I'd better find out exactly 'who' was Roger Moore . . .

Roger Moore

WHEN THE Sainted Bond, called in, I told him bluntly that the part was mine for the asking. Cubby Broccoli and I were in close touch. That was my story. The reality was more like a letter I had had that week from a lady called Betty Collier. It said 'You may wish to be considered for the part of James Bond but how do you expect to cope with the athletic bedroom antics of 007 with your bad back? Don't you think such feats would be beyond your capabilities?'

Sadly I have to agree . . . but what of old Roger Moore? Here he was, still playing Bond, and older than God. Before the show I asked him what he thought of the beautician who had been reported as saying that he had skin that a thousand women would like to touch. How does he keep it in such pristine condition? He answered frankly 'Thick make-up!' But back to Bond – was it really him ski-ing all over Siberia on only one ski . . . ?

What you see, you believe, don't you? You'll believe anything. I'm still fit even if you think I'm too long in the tooth for Bond, but just stretch the imagination. The whole age thing is all you get in the press in England. They can never report anything without mentioning someone's age, like 'A housewife was arrested for shoplifting. Mrs. Brown (aged 48) of . . .'. Can you imagine what it would sound like on TV? I can just see Judith Chalmers at the Bond premiere saying 'Oh yes, and the Prince of Wales, thirty-nine, is coming with his wife the Princess of Wales, twenty-five, in their

margerine
Solid oil
Cat meat 14
Delmonte orange 2
Reet Pepsi Gold
Instant Horlicks
Bunnies
Am plex Deodorant
Toothepaste
Nulon Hand cream
Your loo 5
Lemon Resil
Toi
Kitchen Roll

Mums
prescription
WED

Cards

W/A. Rita+Bob 3rd

" Gaskell 6th

Morris Saladdressing

5th Phyllis H. B/day ₤₤

James o'Daniel 6th.

B/day Rene Muss 8th.

Thurs 29th Aug Harry Jones

Sat 31st Annie Critchley
4 open
2 XW ann
3 ladies B/day

2 men B/day

four-year-old Bentley, driven by twenty-nine-year-old chauffeur . . .' It's hysterical!

Age has nothing to do with my attitude. Obviously I play the part differently to Sean Connery. I came into it after he was very well established. I couldn't play it in the same way. So I had to have a different approach. Anyway, I'm a lighter sort of actor. My only worry about doing it was the comparison with Sean.

I would say to myself 'My name is Bond, James Bond' but I would hear in my mind 'My name is Bond, James Bond' as Sean Connery said it. It was very difficult. But I think we've injected a little more humour. There are more laughs. Bond films are so outrageous, the stunts are outrageous, everything is beyond belief. There is no such thing as a spy who can walk in anywhere in the world and have every bartender recognise him and say 'Ah, Mr. Bond, vodka Martini shaken not stirred'. Spies aren't like that, are they? They're unknown faces that could pass in a crowd and not be noticed. Come to think of it, it could well be a part for Terry Wogan . . .

Don't forget that between Bond films, I've been lucky enough to find producers misguided enough to put up money for me for other films. I take the whole thing of acting quite seriously – well, at least I'm always on time! I figure if I'm not there, somebody else is going to get the part!

On the other hand, I still find making most movies enormous fun. You'd be a bit of a nit not to get any fun out of them. I get overpaid for acting – it's a bit like being an overpaid schoolboy. I can't work in a tight, closed atmosphere. I like it to be relaxed, and have fun! I enjoy myself.

I don't worry too much about the critics. Anyway, a Bond movie is not the sort of film that is going to get a glowing review from the critic who wants to appear to be, let us say, erudite. It's entertainment, pure and simple. It's for people to enjoy themselves. I always say those who can, *do*; those that *can't do* teach; and those who can't do either become critics.

One of my first notices was in *TIME* magazine for a film called *Above The Title* with Lana Turner. It said 'Lana Turner came on to a clattering of high heels and fluttering of false eyelashes followed by a lump of English roast beef'. That was me!

Zsa Zsa Gabor

NATURALLY, I had expected to talk to the distinguished Hungarian philosopher Ms Zsa Zsa Gabor on matters of deep importance. So it was no surprise when she opened her too-brief thesis with a word or two on the vexed subject of morality in the wedded state . . .

I've had eight husbands because I'm very moral. If you're moral you can't live with a man without being married, so I marry them and when I've had enough, I leave. After three years, marriage gets so wobbly. How can you tell what you're going to do tomorrow?

Sexual attraction only lasts two years. Once it lasted four years, and my real husband didn't like it. The biggest luck in the world is to have a marriage which lasts. I was once Hungarian, then I was Turkish, then I was American, then I was English. I've lived in so many countries, it's difficult to last. I am not difficult to live with. I really am a very good housewife. I cook, I love my animals.

But men are impossible. They are unfaithful. When a man has been unfaithful, I don't want him. I think: let him go to the other woman. I've only been unfaithful once. Just once. I couldn't resist him!

I'm a very hard-working woman. I make much money. A man likes a woman to make money. Let's face it, there's no better aphrodisiac than money! I have a couple of houses, I have horses, and dogs. I have a husband, then I'm alone for a couple of years, then I marry again.

It makes my present husband very nervous. He is German. He is a prince, and he decided five years ago he was going to marry me, before knowing me. And at the wedding a Hungarian friend who was giving me away said 'Does Frederick know what he's getting?' I said 'I don't think so.'

I was making a movie in Germany – in Berlin. I got lost. Who the hell knows where Berlin is? I don't. So they took me in a car behind the Berlin Wall. (When you go behind the wall, you don't know you are behind the wall, until you come out. Then you know.) So I'm behind the wall in Potsdam, which I also don't know. The German producer says 'Zsa Zsa Gabor is stupid. She doesn't know where the DDR is.' Thank God I didn't know it. Now I know it. Anyhow, we made a gorgeous film there, even though we were arrested five or six times!

I slept in Weimar, in the Hotel Elephant, in Hitler's bed. The bed had a wooden thing around it. I was black and blue just getting in and out of it. Then there was a bed bug in the bed. It must have been a reincarnation of Hitler because the whole night he was biting me. I had to get up at five o'clock to get to the studio to work, or else.

Everything was *verboten* or *achtung*. I even spoke to six or ten Russian soldiers. Friends said 'Don't you dare talk to them.' I thought what can they do, they can only shoot me. You can only be shot once. These soldiers, the youngest was sixteen, the oldest was twenty-two, they were petrified of talking. I spoke to them in German. They didn't speak German. I spoke a couple of Russian words I had learnt. They smiled, and as you see, didn't kill me at all.

I learnt a little Russian from George Sanders. My present husband is very nice but George Sanders was the great love of my life. He was wonderful. George was an intellectual, and a wonderful, wonderful person. He killed himself, which I can never forgive, because no intelligent man like him should ever kill himself.

To date I have had eight husbands because, I suppose, I'm an incurable romantic. You have to be romantic to survive this world. I like nice people. I'm a very simple woman, I like to cook, I like to horse ride, I like my dogs. I work because I have to pay my bills, damn it. I never had a husband who paid my bills. I married all these rich men and nobody pays nothing. I always pay. Isn't that awful? But I like it, because then you can leave any time you want. The only way you can get rid of a man is if you don't ask for alimony. It's wonderful to catch a man. But it's wonderful to get rid of him!

Roger Vadim

A ND WHAT does the husband of a beautiful woman (or two or three...) think about all this? When Roger Vadim appeared on the show, I'm sure that every male viewer of impressionable age – forty and over – was saying 'What's he got that I haven't'. It's not *what* he's got, it's *who*, really. Brigitte Bardot, Annette Stroyberg, Catherine Deneuve, Jane Fonda. He's loved and lost them all – the lucky boulevardier. He even wrote a book about them.

He let me into a few romantic secrets:

Actually, I don't like living with stars. It's not something I would wish for my best friend. But to live with a very interesting woman before she becomes a star, that is a fascinating experience. I don't regret it, and I wrote the book because I wanted people to share it with me. I'm not selfish.

I did not exploit these women. I think they exploited me. I helped them, and I'm very pleased for their success. I was delighted that they got Oscars, or made money or became the most wonderful actresses in the world. I've helped and was pleased. But nobody has exploited them. They're free. I just helped them. I would have exploited them if I'd had a contract with them, or been their agent, taking ten per cent of what they do. The only thing I did was to help them to become famous.

People say 'You dropped them'. Things are not like that. Each case was different. To love someone needs two persons. To leave someone also usually needs two persons. And things are not that simple. Personally I think I accept Roman Polanski's theory: he said that when men were living in caves they had to protect the babies for four years. The women get pregnant, there is a baby for four years, and after that they are on their own. He said that's when men took the habit of leaving to change women.

The strange thing about my life is that not only have I myself been raising some of the children, particularly the two girls, but they all get on together very well. I see them all the time, and I'm really very close to them. It's bizarre. Some people have children, from the same mother, and they hardly see their children. Each one of mine from a different mother, and I keep them.

However, I do get them slightly confused. Once I put the wrong children on the wrong plane back to the wrong mother! All the planes for Europe were leaving from the same building, and I got a little confused. When I left the building I was called back, and Air France told me: 'I don't think this child was to go to Paris'. I sent the wrong child to the wrong mother! Jane Fonda got my son from Catherine Deneuve, Annette got Natalie – no Christian, from er, er, the other mother. I spent the night calling the mothers. 'Hey listen, sorry, but you're not going to get the right child.'

But I'm not going to get married again. I want to keep some excitement for my next reincarnation!

Joanna Lumley

IN COMMON with the rest of the known male world, I freely admit to a sneaking regard for Joanna Lumley. We are the best of chums but only seem to meet on opposite sides of some outsize charity cheques. So I was more than delighted when, at long last, she agreed to sit in the hot seat. Really and truly the light should have been dimmed to a soft candle-glow and a decent bottle of champagne to hand. As it was, we both had to do some work.

After the usual urbanities, I got down to the serious abuse. Was she busy with her acting and writing and charity work? Anyway, why was it that she didn't stick to anything for very long? Joanna is at her best when she is angry . . .

One of the reasons why one tends not to come on 'Wogan' is that one is abused. It isn't that I don't stick at anything for very long. It's just that I have a lot of interests and I find it terribly difficult just not to be interested in things when they crop up. I love more and more things. I just try to cram them all in, whether it's charity work, writing, acting on TV or acting on the stage.

I am back on the stage now, but I was off it for ten years. I was very busy doing *The Avengers*, *Sapphire and Steel*, and all sorts of other things. Suddenly a play came up and I said 'Yes, I love it.' But I just became afraid. I had viral meningitis, which is a horrible brain disease which rather robs you of the powers of memory. And so I had a fear not only that I would forget my lines and I would dry, but I wouldn't even remember what play I was in! Which could be a distressing evening in the theatre for the audience.

I also have a massive lack of self-confidence. As a child I was very tall, and desperately spotty. I still bear some of the scars. I had beastly frizzly hair and was very disagreeable to look at – an unpleasant-looking girl, though well-meaning. And I was frightfully shy about the way I looked. It sticks with you even when you grow up.

Despite all of this, I eventually agreed to do a play even though I was going through this dreadful period of stage fright. It was just because I had been off the stage for so long. It's the most ghastly feeling, I can tell you: when you know that you have to go on and do the entire play and your heart is hammering. Eventually, I did appear again in front of a speaking, breathing public. I didn't lose my nerve. And now I think it's the greatest fun. I love it.

In fact, I am in a play at the moment at Chichester. I have just travelled to Shepherd's Bush very very quickly to see you, Mr Wogan. I was going to say how fast I had driven but I'd better not. I did drive quickly . . . and I brought my new husband with me.

Tonight, he is following me around. Usually it is I who follow him. I follow him around sort of dog-like. He is a brilliant orchestral conductor. Luckily I love music. I always loved classical music, but I didn't know anything about it. I was a complete amateur. And I knew very little about opera. I'm learning now and it's wonderful.

I think that you only really marry one person and you only marry the right person. And this is the right person. They're not everywhere. They're hard to find. Well, not hard to find. That looks as though you're looking for them. It's just that if you meet somebody who you *must* marry, you *must* marry them. I met Stephen actually a long time before we got married. I met him, and even that was a bit of a bolt from the blue. I met him at somebody else's wedding where he was playing the organ. He's a brilliant organist.

I used to fiddle about on the piano by ear, but now I've got Stephen to play the piano properly at home I don't have to do that. I just say, 'I think a little Chopin' and he can play it.

We kept the wedding pretty much of a secret. We both did that on purpose because the press have slightly changed their complexion, I think, over the last five years. They tend not to be just agreeable monitors of what's going on, but they like to take things in their own hands and put a slant on things. And on very important occasions you don't really want a slant.

In the old days you had to give a lot of interviews. They always wanted to know something about your private life. So I'd say 'I can't really answer that, but I've got a wonderful recipe for yoghurt make-up.' And they'd sort of go 'Oh yes, do tell me.' I'd say 'Well, you get a pot of yoghurt . . .' and come out with some awful recipe which was completely made up, and they'd feel they had an answer. This went on for years. I used to lie, which was wrong. I told them I was building a four-poster bed in the garage – I didn't even have a garage. But that appeared in the cuttings for a long time. I've stopped lying now. I just avoid the press.

That evening I sipped my usual champagne in the hospitality room, while Joanna's husband moodily tinkled the odd etude or prelude on the white pianoforte.
you very much. Thank you.

Spike Milligan

WHEN I heard Spike Milligan was going to leave the country for good, I thought it was just another merry quip from our most senior and legendary buffoon. But no, it turned out to be true – at least for the duration of one 'Wogan'. Bill Wyman had been collecting farewell autographs for him, in secret, and wanted to present them to him on the show. First though, I had to ask Spike exactly why he was leaving and where he was going:

I'm travelling to the Australias. There's no work here, so I thought I'd go out there. They want me to go out there to do a show, and I found there was a Polish ship called the *Gdansk* going. It used to be called the *Marie Celeste*.

I went to have a look at it. They said there were a few bits missing off it. I said 'Like what?' They said 'Like the crew'. And the captain worried me, because he'd just retired from Alcoholics Anonymous. So they're worried about him, because every night he sleeps in the lifeboat. I'm very worried about this Polish line because when I booked a ticket, they sent me an oar in return.

I am looking forward to seeing my mother. She lives in Australia. (You don't look backward to see your mother, of course). She's an old lady. (She used to be an old man, but things changed.) I sold my house to some Japanese, believe it or not. But I've had it mined – so that on the anniversary of Pearl Harbour the whole place goes up.

I must tell you about this Japanese bloke who jumped ship in

Dublin. They gave him a job in an Irish coal mine. They said 'Do you speak English?' He said 'No, no speak English.' They said 'Well, you look after supplies.' He said 'OK.' And suddenly he went missing. They started looking for him, and after forty-eight hours, he jumped from behind a pit prop and went 'Supplise!'

I must tell you, this could only happen in Ireland. I went to a hotel in Dublin last week, where I was doing a show. I said to the waiter, 'Can you leave me a meal upstairs after the show?' He said 'I'll do it, I'll do that, sir.' I came back, and as I was going up to my room, he's wheeling the meal in. I noticed there were two dinners on it. He said 'I thought there was two of you.' I said 'No, there's always only been one of me.' He said 'Shall I leave the extra meal, or shall I take it away?' I said 'Have you had dinner?' He said 'No.' I said 'Would you like this?' So he sat down and had dinner with me. I said 'What do you think of it?' He said 'Oh, with your money I'd have ordered a better meal than that.'!

Just before we left Ireland, two Irish teams were playing football. (This happened last week.) Twenty minutes before the end, one team said 'We've got to go now. The last train leaves in a few minutes.' So this team left the field. But the referee blew his whistle and play went on with one team. The opposition team were losing up to then. They obviously scored a goal and won. That's how it is in Ireland.

Now as a surprise to Spike I introduced Bill Wyman, who along with Steve Blacknall, had been collecting Spike's bon-voyage messages in a book. He came on to the show to present Spike with the book:

SPIKE: This must be a joke – I'm sorry

WYMAN: We didn't want you to go, and you'd better come back. This is from about 250 people who love you.

WOGAN: Everybody's in there. Famous people, all sorts. Messages. From them all.

SPIKE: Like don't come back. I know. Nobody needs me here, that's why I'm going away. But thank you. I'm astounded. I can't believe this.

WOGAN: Everyone's here in the book. Alec Guiness, Albert Finney . . . Everyone.

SPIKE: I can't believe this. I'll have these valued tomorrow. This is marvellous. Here's Albert Finney – 'Spike. The audition may be tough, but they can't do the show without you.'

WYMAN: They're your mates. Keith Richards wrote a good one. 'To Spike. If they don't give you a passport, I'll lend you mine.'

WOGAN: Denis Healey drew himself and said 'Don't be a silly billy'. Here's Mel Brooks – 'Any nation should be privileged to have you as one of their own. So fiercely talented, so so funny. And not even a Jew.'

SPIKE: You realise you've ruined my ad libbing now. I'm speechless now. I don't know what to say. I really am a very profound person. I cover myself up like a child with jokes. And I'm pretty overwhelmed by this, and all I can say is one word – thank you very much. Thank you.

After all that, he kept us entertained well into the evening in the hospitality room, or hostility as it's come to be called by those of us who've been there before. But a few days later we heard another rumour: Spike Milligan was not going anywhere after all. He had changed his mind. Watch this space.

Dallas

Victoria Principal

I'VE BEEN with 'Dallas' since the very beginning, and it hasn't been easy, I can tell you. We've been through dungeon, fire and sword together, the Ewings and me: I remember Digger Barnes, Lusty Dusty the eight-egg omelette man, the Poison Dwarf, the two Miss Ellies. I mind well the day Jock's copter went down, and the night Bing Crosby's daughter shot J.R. Even now, my mind races at the mention of wire coat-hangers, wind on the patio, and breakfasts where people pile their plates with ham and eggs, and then never eat a thing . . .

One thing you could be sure of in 'Dallas' was that you could never be sure of anything. Least of all the one thing we're all supposed to be certain of – death. 'The dead arise and appear to many' in 'Dallas'. I should have known at the time I talked to Victoria Principal that Bobby Ewing wasn't *really* dead. However, she didn't know it either, at the time. So the poor distracted woman accused *me* of being behind all the carnage . . .

On the night that Bobby was killed off, I was joined by Victoria Principal.

VICTORIA PRINCIPAL: Let me tell you something. You really have the evil eye! I don't want you to make any jokes about me in 'Dallas', because last time, you made jokes about Charlene, and jokes about what you called my 'ugly baby', and now they're both gone. You did it! You're so cruel! You're so bad! We're going to have you on 'Dallas' as a hit man.

WOGAN: We're looking forward to a real weepie on 'Dallas'. The final episode. We know that something terrible is going to happen, and a woman in a blonde wig is going to do it. With long red fingernails. It's not you in drag, is it?

VICTORIA: You're terrible!

WOGAN: Are you going to do a lot of acting in this? Or will you just be yourself?

VICTORIA: Actually, I do some rather credible work in this episode.

WOGAN: Steady! Who else acts well? Does Bobby act good, or is a lot of it immobile?

VICTORIA: He acts as always. After being married to Patrick Duffy for seven years on the programme it's not quite the same for me. I miss his presence every day.

WOGAN: When I talked to the 'Dynasty' people here, they all said they couldn't stand you.

VICTORIA: No they didn't! You're so bad! Listen, what did you do to Joan Rivers? She hasn't been the same since she saw you.

WOGAN: She won't talk to me now. At least you'll talk to me. You're one of the very few people in America who speak to me.

VICTORIA: I suppose that speaks well of me.

WOGAN: Probably shows a weakness of character. But I like that in a woman.

Patrick Duffy

WHEN PATRICK DUFFY (Bobby Ewing) joined me he had already left 'Dallas'. American audiences had seen the bloody massacre – we hadn't. He had yet to realise that of course it was all a dream and he would come back. But first I had to get one or two vital questions out of the way:

WOGAN: How tall are you?

PATRICK DUFFY: Six three.

WOGAN: Six three of bone and muscle

DUFFY: – and padding, and special effects.

WOGAN: The old plastic surgery?

DUFFY: No, no. Not yet. I'm only 36. When I'm 37, it all gets tightened up.

WOGAN: Do you get on with J.R. – Larry Hagman – in real life?

DUFFY: Actually we do. We get all our hate out on the air. I grab his shirt and I get all those little chest hairs in my hands . . .

WOGAN: Just settle another thing. How big is the pool at Southfork?

DUFFY: We have two pools. We have one that we built on the sound stage, which is only four foot deep. So whenever we're swimming and no one's diving, we're on the sound stage.

WOGAN: We've noticed the gale force winds – does the sun ever shine in Dallas, or is it just those steely grey skies and the wind all the time?

DUFFY: The sun shines, and the winds blow. We call that wind 'horizontal coffee' wind. You're pouring your coffee and it pours out sideways right across the table!

WOGAN: Why did you decide to give the elbow to the part of Bobby? Is he definitely out for good?

DUFFY: I can definitely say *if* Bobby survives his accident, that he will come back looking like someone else.

WOGAN: Old Mama, she leaves as one person, then she comes back as someone else. And now she's coming back again. Can you stand it?

DUFFY: Well, instead of saying 'Where's Mama?' we say 'Who's Mama?' But seriously I have left, and I asked them very poignantly, I felt, not to replace me with somebody else. I really want to go out befitting the hero that I created for seven years.

WOGAN: Is the production company very considerate of your wishes and feelings in the matter of the characters that you play?

DUFFY: What they do is they very patiently listen to everything that you say, and do it their way. The producer generally sets the tone on the show. He is very open to suggestions if he feels they're going to be productive and help the show. We have said things and asked if things can be changed, and he's been very open to that. But in terms of saying 'I won't do this or that' or 'This character wouldn't do it', they'll say 'Yes, this character will do it, and if he doesn't do it as a tall dark guy, he'll do it as a short blonde guy.' You know pretty well where the power lies.

WOGAN: One of the things I would get fed up with being Bobby is that he gets all the best-looking women. Was it not a constant temptation to you on the set?

DUFFY: Those two women are not my type of women. My wife of the last thirteen years is a very petite blonde ex-ballerina, and she pushes all the right buttons and rings all the right chimes.

Somehow Victoria and Priscilla, although they're good friends of mine, and they certainly have the equipment – it's just work. When you're lying in bed with Victoria Principal, you look around and there are forty people watching you. At the end of the scene they hold up a 9-5, 9-4, 9-2 . . .

It's not that terrific. It is work.

Howard Keel

WHO WOULD have thought that one of my favourite singers – the man who set the West End on fire in *Oklahoma* – would end up every week trying to remember what the woman he married looks like? But that's just what Clayton Farlow does!

KEEL: They signed me to do two episodes and I've been there ever since. I was still singing. But in this business you have to have visibility every once in a while. You have to go out and create a new audience for yourself. 'Dallas' has been wonderful to me. Old Clay is kind of old Texas clay you know. He has to face up to anything, that boy. Even Miss Ellie completely changing.

There's not much of me in him. But he has the patience of Job. He's a very kind man, I think. But he's not very bright. He's got a lot of money, but you don't have to be real bright to get a lot of money.

WOGAN: Tell me, is it one big happy family in 'Dallas', or is there a certain amount of clash of ego?

KEEL: Some of the cast on 'Dallas' make more money than others, but I'll say this – Larry Hagman is a wonderful person. He's crazy, he's bonkers, he's an eccentric. He's terribly funny, a wonderful actor. Larry has never pulled any star stuff on anyone. He really is the star of the show.

WOGAN: Why does all the action take place over meals, when you never eat anything?

KEEL: No, we don't. The continuity girl goes crazy. You take a bite, you gotta remember when you took the bite, what words, that sort of thing. If you sit down with Pat Duffy, who plays Bobby, and Larry, at a meal like that, it's like sitting down with two of the worst brats in the neighbourhood. They pull more stick at that table. They send the scripts up. It's pandemonium. It's a minor miracle that anything gets done.

Linda Gray

S UE ELLEN – 'Swellen' – the lady who has been in and
out of love, in and out of jail, in and out of hospital and in
and out of the bottle . . . I asked – what else could possibly
happen to the poor girl?

LINDA GRAY: I hope, everything. I'm having the best time of
my life. It's wonderful that one can survive all of that, but I think as
an actress I'd be bored to death if I had to be nice for nine years.

WOGAN: Whenever she's in trouble, though, she either goes to
the bottle or she has an affair?

LINDA: That always seems to be the two storylines that the
writers have chosen for me. It's written by a man, produced by a
man, and men seem to be the focal points, so when they think of a
woman they think a woman does one of two things when she has a
bit of trouble. She drinks or she has an affair. I kept saying to them,
'Excuse me, but this is the 1980's. Other things *do* happen.' It's
about time she had her own life.

WOGAN: What was J.R. like when you started the series? How
did he treat you to begin with?

LINDA: The very first time Larry and I worked together we had
a scene to do and I was supposed to hold up a black teddy. He
looked at me and said 'Take it back to the store. It isn't working.'
That was our very first scene, as Mr. and Mrs. J.R. Ewing in a mini-
series. So when we finished the scene, it was about eight o'clock at

night, and we had worked all day long. He looked at me and said, 'That was terrible. You were terrible. The first time we're Mr. and Mrs. Ewing and you were awful.' And I remember he drove me back to the hotel and I was just sitting there quietly, thinking 'Oh my God, I was awful'. So I got over that and I thought 'I'll be better'. So about seven years later, I was reminding him of this, and I said 'Did you mean that?' He said, 'Oh no. I just wanted you to know who was boss!'

WOGAN: You came into acting late, didn't you? You were in your late twenties before you decided to act?

LINDA: Well, because it was not accepted. I was raised in a very traditional home where it was acceptable for me to be a lawyer or doctor, something professional like that, but it wasn't accepted to go to your parents and say 'I want to become an actress'.

WOGAN: What was your first part?

LINDA: I think I was the Virgin Mary about twelve times in Catholic school. Then I was a daisy.

WOGAN: You have changed!

LINDA: Then I got into television. I did hundreds of commercials. And that was accepted.

WOGAN: And also you've directed a couple of episodes?

LINDA: Yes. They didn't want me to direct. They said 'We can't let *her* direct'. That devastated me. Then Larry came to my defence. He said 'What do you mean, you can't let *her* direct? Yes, we can.' So he was very instrumental. It's a family affair. We all get along. We all make the same decisions. It's just that he makes more decisions than others!

Larry Hagman

FINALLY, INEVITABLY, Bad Ol' J.R. Hisself. It's not
easy to distinguish where J.R. Ewing finishes, and Larry
Hagman begins. Or vice versa. But without both, or either,
'Dallas' wouldn't mean a thing. Hagman is a consummate
actor. If he'd been doing in a feature-length movie what he
does week in and week out on the box, he would have won an
Oscar years ago. He's an ebullient extrovert with some care-
fully-contrived eccentricities. If you smoke near him, he'll
bring out a little electric fan and blow your fumes back in your
face. He claims never to speak on Sunday, and calls himself
'The Mad Monk of Malibu'. Crazy like a fox, that's ol' J.R.

WOGAN: Do you think J.R.'s a successful businessman? It
seems to me if you really tot up how he's done, he's probably lost
the Ewings millions.

LARRY HAGMAN: Absolutely. A couple of years ago we
figured out that he had lost over sixteen million dollars in the last
six years. Taxable dollars. How much untaxable dollars I don't
know.

WOGAN: How much of a hand have you had in turning him into
the kind of character that he is? Was he always supposed to be like
that?

HAGMAN: Well, everybody was supposed to be like that,
originally in the show. Everybody was on the take and fooling

74

around and so forth. But it kind of melted down, filtered down to me.

WOGAN: You were born in Texas. What were you like as a child?

HAGMAN: Oh, honest, truthful, reverent.

WOGAN: Didn't you want to be a cowboy?

HAGMAN: Yes, I did. Then I found out that cowboys dug ditches and cesspools and baled hay and never got to ride a horse. It just wasn't worth it. I figured there was a better way of making a buck than doing that.

WOGAN: Did you model yourself on anybody in particular?

HAGMAN: Sure did. No names. They're still alive.

WOGAN: Do you remember your first stage appearance?

HAGMAN: Yes I do. I was about five. I was playing the woodman in *Red Riding Hood*. And I came out on stage, and I had a little axe. I balanced it on my nose and didn't say any of the lines, like I sometimes don't now. At the end of the performance, everybody got a candy bar – except me, because I didn't do anything they told me to. But now it's paid off, and they pay me more than a candy bar!

WOGAN: 'Dallas' is now seen worldwide. Do you get feedback from weird places?

HAGMAN: Sure, yes, Japanese, Chinese, Italian – I'm very good in Italian. I'm better in Italian than I am in English.

WOGAN: What's J.R. like in Italian?

HAGMAN: Oh he's wonderful. He has a great voice. And he makes it so important and he sounds very romantic. He is wonderful.

WOGAN: You cracked the old whip, didn't you, about bringing back Bobby?

HAGMAN: No, not at all. My *modus operandi* was to get the show back to where it was a year ago.

75

WOGAN: Because it had slumped in the ratings?

HAGMAN: Well, no. It wasn't any fun any more. The ratings can come and go but if there's no fun, there's no sense in doing it. Ratings do have a little to do with it, I suppose. I wanted the show to be successful *and* fun. And that's where I *encouraged* people to make the right decisions.

WOGAN: Were you happy with that dream sequence? I don't know about the American public, but the British public had difficulties accepting that the previous series they'd seen had all been a dream.

HAGMAN: Would you have had him come out of plastic surgery as somebody else?

WOGAN: Everybody comes out of plastic surgery as somebody else.

HAGMAN: He needed to come back as Bobby Ewing. Think about the alternatives, there aren't very many. We had to keep the storyline that we'd established for that whole year going, with all those other people. It would have been very difficult to make it work any other way. Anyhow, it's worked. Like Mama went away and she came back. That worked. Bobby went away, and he came back.

WOGAN: And Danny went away and he's coming back.

HAGMAN: Danny went away and he *ain't* coming back!

WOGAN: Do you miss being a comedy actor?

HAGMAN: Well, I consider myself a comedy actor now. Some of the things we do on 'Dallas' are very funny, if you ask me.

As I write, the BBC are repeating 'Dallas' – the early years. I've always said that J.R. Ewing will dance on all our graves.

Jackie Collins and Barbara Cartland

ONE OF the most explosive encounters on 'Wogan' was when the queen of all those sexy books like *The Stud, Hollywood Husbands* and *Hollywood Wives* – Jackie Collins – came face to face with the queen of romance, Barbara Cartland. At some time in the past, each had reviewed the other's books and they didn't waste much time in having a very public disagreement not only about the relative literary merit of the other's writing but about how they treated the age-old story of sex. I might as well have not been there. Barbara began calmly enough . . .

BARBARA CARTLAND: One of my great things is that we must use the brains and experiences of old people. We don't. We shut them up in homes. I have lots of energy because I keep working. I talked to Zsa Zsa Gabor's eighth husband the other day, and I said, 'Why is Zsa Zsa so wonderful at 68?' and he said 'I'll tell you exactly. She gets up at five o'clock every morning' – nice for him, I thought – 'and she swims for two hours and then she's go, go, go all day.'

So that's the answer – go, go, go all day. You've got to keep going. Once you sit down to think about yourself, then you'll die. People die of boredom. Nobody ever died of work.

Lord Grade, who is 80, has seen the mess of the permissive society, and seen how we've got to go back to the family. That's why he's going to make one of my books into a television series. It's the first, because in the past my books were too pure, you see.

Everyone wanted something dirty – people rolling about naked on beds. So now at last Lord Grade has realised that we've got to go back to the family to save the world.

I mean, look at the mess we're in. The permissive society has failed utterly. We've got Aids, we've got everything that's awful and we've got children more badly treated than they've ever been in history. We've got to try and do something about it. It's evil really – and so are the books you write, Jackie. Have you ever thought of the effect they have on young people?

JACKIE COLLINS: Yes, they love it. Every moment of it. They write me letters and say 'I was reading it under the covers and matron came in and said "What are you reading?".'. Let me tell you, Barbara, there's room for both of us. There's room for your books, and there's room for mine, which are a little more racy.

BARBARA: But don't you think they have helped the perverts? For instance, there is all this awful abuse of children. All that comes from the permissive society. Everybody said to me, 'You're the queen of romance. We're all going to enjoy romance.' But they didn't get romance. Authors in America were told to write like Barbara Cartland with pornography. I went to America and there all the middle-aged women were writing about awful things they knew nothing about.

JACKIE: Nobody has ever said to me 'You must write like Barbara with pornography'.

BARBARA: No, no, because you've done it on your own.

JACKIE: There's a question I've been meaning to ask. A newspaper did a piece on Barbara once, and a piece on me. And Barbara was given *The Stud* to read. And she said 'It's a horrible disgusting book, and I stayed up all night reading it.' I want to know what she was doing all night.

BARBARA: I never said that at all.

JACKIE: You did.

BARBARA: I said, yours is a horrible book because it is so terribly improper. You see, I worry terribly about the people who

78

follow us. Nobody has really worked out what happens when that sort of thing goes into the brain. You can't get rid of it.

JACKIE: Barbara, you said something very interesting. (I'm sorry, Terry, I do know this is your show!) But Barbara said something very interesting about 'All these people rolling around naked on beds, it's disgusting'. I really don't think there's anything disgusting about people rolling about naked on beds. I thought that was what you were supposed to do when you're married.

BARBARA: Love is quite different to what we've had. We've had sex, sex, sex. When our romantic era came in, everybody said, 'Now we're going to have every sort of sex.' There was nothing about love in it at all. It was just animal lust.

JACKIE: Have you read *Hollywood Wives?*

BARBARA: No, thank you.

JACKIE: It's difficult to criticise when you haven't read it.

BARBARA: No, well, I criticised *The Stud*, and I've read and criticised the advertisements on your books you put in America. You put 'Barbara Cartland with iron knickers'.

JACKIE: I didn't.

WOGAN: This woman is innocent. We have to take her word for it. What I would like to know is have you read any of Barbara's books?

JACKIE: I did, and it reminded me very much of Enid Blyton.

BARBARA: I loved Enid Blyton. I read every book to my children.

JACKIE: I think there is a place for everybody. There's a place for Barbara's books and there's a place for my books. I would never criticise Barbara and I would never say all books have to be like hers, because wouldn't life be dull if we all had to do the same thing?

BARBARA: I said, we've all got to think today of what effect we're having on other people. We do have a responsibility to our audience, and we've really got to think of the young people coming

79

up. I'm old. I shall be dead. You'll be going on long after me. We know immorality has gone too far – you can't say it hasn't. We've got to go back and bring out the right moral ideas for young people.

JACKIE: I have to tell you, Terry, I'm enjoying this. Best fun I've had on a television show in a long time. You usually sit there and you're boringly polite. This is good, really good.

Paul Hogan

W E DON'T have many Australians on 'Wogan' (the
'Wogan' budget only stretches to a tandem to and from
Highbury), but one was unforgettable – and yes, Paul Hogan
drank the amber nectar in 'hostility'. He told us a few things
we didn't know too!

I had a terrific start. I was a rigger on Sydney Harbour Bridge.
Nothing to do with show business, but it's what I did for a living.
There used to be a show on called 'New Faces', like 'Opportunity
Knocks', and it was dreadful. You used to get these professional
entertainers of dubious talent telling the amateurs where they were
going wrong. It was aggravating, because they used to humiliate
these poor little kids. So we used to sit around at work saying
'Someone should go on and take the mickey out of those guys' and
being 'someone' was always my forte.

So I went on. I wrote them a letter and said I was a tap-dancing
knife-thrower. I knew they wouldn't be able to resist that. I could
neither tap-dance nor throw a knife. So I went on with a big pair of
wellies and a dustbin over my head, with half a dozen large knives. I
just went on and ripped into the judges. They had a gong then to
get rid of people, but they weren't game to gong me. Well, with a
handful of knives you wouldn't, would you? So I sort of took over
that show.

It went on from there. They said, you've got to come back. I
thought, what am I going to do next time? So I came back as a
shovel player. Then a thunderbox player – two tea chests nailed

together. All I did was I came on and talked about whatever I wanted to talk about, and right at the end of the act ran across the stage and drove my head right through the side.

Over here, I suppose I am more known for the lager commercials. And I am genuinely confused about British life. I've been coming here for a while, and this is a weird country. It's the home of dingbats and eccentrics and everything. That's not abuse. It's wonderful and I love it. I think dingbats make the world go round. If I came all the way across to here and found out it was full of sensible, down-to-earth normal people like myself, I'd be bored and I'd go back home. But I come here and see the weirdos, and I think it's great.

I think the Royals are fabulous. I get annoyed when you say you spend too much money on them, because believe me, we'd have them like a flash. If you get bored with your Royals, we'll give you Ayers Rock or Rolf Harris. Poor Charles, for instance, he's destined for two things from the moment he's born. He can either be adequate or inadequate. He can't be a brilliant king. No one will ever say, 'Young Charlie's done well.' Where can you go after king?

But the funniest thing about the English is the funny haircuts. Men sometimes go bald, they go bald in Australia – I'm getting a bit thin on top – so you comb your hair over the bald spot till it's too late, then you give up. In America you get a toupee or a transplant. But the Englishman has invented more ways of covering his head than I would have thought possible. There's one man I saw here on TV (and I don't want to get involved in your politics). He's called Arthur Scargill. I don't know what he does for a living, but I reckon he grows his hair out of his ears and combs it over his head!

Still, to you I'm a foreigner – something the Brits invented. Everyone who isn't English is a foreigner. I suppose they invented me too. After all, they sent my ancestors out to Australia in chains!

Arthur Scargill

P AUL HOGAN may not know what Arthur does for a
living, but media coverage has ensured that most people
in the British Isles do, and most of them have a particular
picture of the man. Guests on 'Wogan', however, often show
a different side to themselves and Arthur Scargill was one
such. Not at all the demagogue you might have expected. Our
conversation concentrated not on the politics of the National
Union of Mineworkers but on the difference between the
image of the ranter seen on TV and the man. Even Arthur
must have quiet moments?

Time and time again when I meet people, they say 'You're totally
different to the bloke we thought you were.' That demonstrates to
me very clearly that they look at someone not as they are but
judging them on the basis of the image on television, radio or in the
newspapers. I usually get interviewed in a very abrasive fashion,
and respond equally, and people judge me on that basis. It's very
rare that I'm able to expand on other issues. For example, I'm not
able to talk about nuclear power, or issues of the Third World, and
I'm not able to talk about my other involvements in life.

I understand that the media, particularly in this country, will
paint me as the devil incarnate, because to paint me in any other
way would be to give me some kind of credibility from their point
of view. What usually happens is that they film a speech of about 45
minutes, and they'll take a clip of about twenty seconds and put it
on national television. Or put a photograph where I'm waving to a

crowd and try to portray that as a sign that would be given in Nazi Germany. That's about the farthest thing from what I would ever do. Now, if you get that sort of image portrayed either on TV or radio or in the newspapers, you'll obviously convince people that the person you're attacking is all bad.

I've often contrasted my image with soap operas like 'Coronation Street', or episodes of 'The Forsyte Saga'. I remember my wife and daughter absolutely detesting Soames in 'The Forsyte Saga', until one episode his wife left him, and he became a figure of great sympathy. It suddenly changed their attitude towards him. I said 'But he's exactly the same bloke he was last week.' 'No, it's different,' they said. What they were really saying was it was a different image that was being painted of the person in that particular episode. And it's the same with me. I think if people listen to me a little while, listen to what I've got to say about issues that are of vital importance, then they might get a different opinion.

I think that people do things that they believe are right. It may be that they're wrong. But if you honestly believe that what you're doing is right, then you should do it. If I didn't think I was right, I wouldn't be doing the job I'm doing. And I happen to think that it's right, for example, to campaign against nuclear power stations. I think it's right that we should say the Russians are wrong, the Americans are wrong and the Britons are wrong to pursue a policy which could cause catastrophe for all of us. In that, other people don't agree with me. But as far as I'm concerned, I believe I'm right.

I've often said, ever since I was about 13 or 14, I couldn't understand a world where on the one hand we've massive amounts of wheat and beef and butter, and on the other hand we've got starving children in Ethiopia and the Sudan. Why on earth they can't put one with the other escaped me then and still escapes me now.

As President of the National Union of Mineworkers, I am able to influence policies not only in the Trade Union but in the Labour Party. I've been offered at least four Member of Parliament jobs over the past ten years. But really, when you come to think of it, if you ask who was the MP for such-and-such constituency, you have to think very hard. If you ask who's the President of the NUM, by and large most people will know.

I like the power of being able to settle and win things for people. Many of the things that I do never hit the headlines, never get the front page of, say, the *Daily Express* or the *Daily Mail*. I remember settling a Common Law damages case that gave me a great deal of satisfaction. It was for five paraplegic mineworkers – a case that had gone on for twenty-three years. I walked into a home one night and this woman asked me what progress had been made. I said 'What would you say if I said we could settle it out of court?' and she said 'Mr. Scargill, if someone would give us a thousand pounds, I'd think someone cared. And for the first time my husband and myself and the family could go on holiday together.' When I handed that woman £25,000, the look on her husband's face and on her face made my job worthwhile. They said a lot about my job that made me proud to be President of the NUM at that time. But that will never hit the headlines.

I'll tell you what I want. I want to see every child in Britain grow up to have the right to have a job. A moderate demand. I want to see every child in the world free from the horror of nuclear war. A moderate view. I'm the most remarkably modest man you could meet. I'm a moderate Yorkshireman.

Placido Domingo

I T WAS, of course, a pleasure to welcome Placido Domingo – one of the giants of opera and a man with a mission to make it as popular as possible. Concerts in the park . . . giant television screens – where will it all end?

At Covent Garden, we have had a big screen outside in the piazza and surtitles – the words over the stage – the translation. I do think that it helps. If people know their opera very well, then they shouldn't look at them – just concentrate on what is going on on stage. But some people don't know what is going on, they only like the music. They can get a lot more involved in the drama if they are able to see what is happening. Then they can appreciate it a lot more – not only your acting, but what you sing. They see your reactions, even at the moment you sing certain words.

Opera, I hope, is becoming more popular. In the next month, besides two performances in Covent Garden, with a big outdoor screen in the piazza, I am giving a performance of *Tosca* in Central Park in New York for something like 600,000 to 800,000 people. Then I am giving a performance at Wembley, for nine or ten thousand people, then in Israel a concert for 350,000 people. And then I go to Spain, my own country, for three performances of *Carmen*, in the bullring for 15,000 people each performance. So I am always looking to really be able to bring music to more and more people. And in most places it will be free. Central Park is for free. Israel is also free.

I know I once disappointed a lot of people by not appearing.

86

This is a kind of way of making up. It was always my idea to do that particular concert, but not in those circumstances and not at that moment. I am not sorry for what I did because I would do it again if the circumstances were the same. But of course I apologise to the people, for their expenses and so on. But I hope I can make up for it.

I have made three films of three great operas: *Traviata*, *Carmen* and *Othello*. They have been very, very popular, one perhaps more than the others. It is not instant popularity, but it is something that stays there forever. It can come back after five years. The public will always go to see that film.

Today, we have opera singers not only from Italy, but from all around the world. Especially from the Eastern countries, a lot of Bulgarians and from Hungary. And we have an Australian. So you have great great singers, international singers. The only Italian in the cast is the conductor. But there are great Italian singers all around the world, of course.

Italian opera-house audiences are amazing. Let me tell you something. When I arrived in Verona, somebody came and said 'How do you like it?' I said, 'Fine, fantastic.' 'Do you like the public?' I said, 'Sure. Fantastic. Twenty thousand people.' He said, 'We did a good job.' I said, 'What do you mean, a good job?' He said, 'Yes, we were backing you there.' I said, 'Who is "we"?' He said, 'My people and me.' I said, 'My God, that's a big group! There were twenty thousand cheering there.'

There are certain theatres where the claque is an institution. I have been fighting it. The public has to react. In La Scala today, the public sits in the stalls, and sometimes they don't know what to do. They watch the people upstairs – they don't know what to do, applaud or disapprove. The people in the stalls are just the normal people, and they don't know how to react. So these claques are very bad.

Julie Andrews

AFTER *Mary Poppins, The Sound of Music* and *Thoroughly Modern Millie*, she was voted quite simply the most popular star in the entire world. With a person like Julie Andrews, what you see is what you get. She's charming, vivacious, witty. A far cry from the humble beginnings of playing stooge to a ventriloquist's dummy! Julie began her career as Archie Andrews' sister before spreading her wings . . .

I was seven when I started singing. When I really started working hard, I was about twelve. I travelled so much it seemed a good idea that, rather than try to fit into various schools, I would have a governess who travelled with me. She put up with a lot of flak and problems, but she was a wonderful lady. In those days I was spoiled. I had a wonderful time and I was made to feel special. On the one hand, I missed school friends. But on the other I learned so much. It was a very odd education, especially since I was always on the move.

It was Hattie Jacques who was instrumental in getting my first break. She was with me in the 'Educating Archie' series with the famous dummy. And I was also performing in *Cinderella* at the Palladium. The lady that was directing *The Boyfriend* on Broadway was looking for someone to play the lead and Hattie Jacques very sweetly said 'Why don't you go and see young Julie Andrews at the Palladium?' She did, and I was plunged over to Broadway at a tender age. I knew I would be desperately homesick. In fact, I was very homesick. But my father said 'Look, it could last three weeks. You could be home very quickly. Go and open up your head. It will do you good.' It did.

Then of course I got taken up for the part of Eliza Doolittle in *My Fair Lady*. I was just terrible, and very out of my depth, very green. I had a feeling that if only somebody would work with me I could do it. I knew that. I don't think anybody else did, except our director, Moss Hart – I shall be forever grateful to him. He suggested that he and I just worked together for a while. And he showed me how to be Eliza. He bullied, he pleaded, he cajoled, and after 48 hours he'd really shaped me into Eliza Doolittle.

At the end of this incredible 48 hours he went home to his wife who said 'How was she?' He said 'Oh, she's much better. She has that terrible British strength that makes you wonder why they lost India!'

I have happy memories of all my films but my most vivid memory from *The Sound of Music* was shooting that wonderful walk across the fields. The shot was from a helicopter, and the camera was hanging out of the side of it. This huge helicopter came sort of crab-wise towards me and I walked from one end of the field to the other to meet it. We would meet in the middle. Then when he'd finished the take, he would circle right round and go back to his point and I'd rush back to mine and we'd do it all over again. Just to be sure we had it. This went on about ten or fifteen times, and every single time the helicopter circled around me, the downdraught from the jet of the helicopter just levelled me flat in the field. I just kept being knocked out. I got so mad at it!

It was because of these parts in *Mary Poppins* and *The Sound Of Music*, that people say I have a very goody-goody image. But I don't knock the image because it did give so many people so much pleasure. The thing about image is you're remembered for the films that are best known, and certainly the *Sound of Music* and *Mary Poppins* were such huge successes that I think people were apt to forget that they were roles and not a person.

The goody-goody image went out of the window, though, for *S.O.B.* It was a film in which I had to appear topless. The film on the whole was fun to make (depending on whether it was chilly or not!). Then one of my most demanding parts, I think, was in *Duet For One*. I only had about four or five weeks to learn to look as though I could play the violin. I made my debut at the Albert Hall in front of an entire Symphony Orchestra. That takes a bit of guts, I can tell you! There I was, sawing away, trying to look like I'd been playing the violin for twenty years. The real violinists in the orchestra were very supportive and very dear. I got a thumbs up from them so I guess I was all right.

In *Duet For One* I play a person who suffers from multiple sclerosis. So I consulted all the people who knew all about it. (Acting is hard work sometimes.) I went to a wonderful clinic for MS in Bromley and talked to all the people there. They were very, very helpful. It was a very tough film for me to do. There was a lot to remember, a lot to do, and it was very sad. But it was wonderful to do.

But whatever the parts, I think I'm very fortunate that all these things have come my way. I'm very grateful for that. For my next film, I think a wonderful musical would be nice to do!

Sara Keays

THE VERY name of Sara Keays seems to polarise the entire population. There is nobody who hasn't an opinion on the lady, and there appear to be only two sides to the argument: (a) she is a vengeful harridan who nearly destroyed a promising politician's career and marriage; (b) she is a woman who has been cruelly wronged, seeking her just deserts. In the opinion of the Great British Public, there are no grey areas between the black and the white.

WOGAN: Are you still angry about what happened, or angry about what you have said to be a media bias against you?

SARA KEAYS: I am rather depressed by the endless repetition of the misapprehensions and downright lies that circulated in 1983, which are repeated to this very day – principally that it was I who brought the whole matter into the public domain, and it was I who caused the scandal to burst upon the public, when it was not.

WOGAN: Do you blame the media, or the Tory Party Central Office? Who's behind it?

SARA: I blame the Conservative Party for the fact it developed in the way it did. I feel that the initial error of judgement by the Prime Minister enabled all the other things to follow and that if Cecil Parkinson had not taken an appointment in her new government in June 1983, then the scandal would have been minimised. I think we all would have been spared a great deal of suffering and he would be in the government now.

WOGAN: Do you think that your very reticence about the Cecil Parkinson affair has worked against you? That perhaps you haven't been forceful enough about that?

SARA: No. I don't think it's anybody's business. Those sort of details are not relevant. All I was concerned to do was defend my reputation against the most frightful things which were said about me and which started with a whispering campaign which was, if not actually initiated by No.10 Downing Street, certainly done with its blessing. I think some of the rumours actually started there. I endured the resulting media coverage and things which were said about me and my family for nearly two years and decided then that I had to put a stop to it. The only thing I have done to clear my name is to write a book . . . It's about judgement, personal and political judgement, but principally about political judgement.

WOGAN: There was a question mark over the timing of the various accusations that you had made. They seemed to work against Mr. Parkinson's further advancement.

SARA: There's been a lot of nonsense talked about timing. If people really believe that I set out to harm him or harm the Conservative Party, then they should ask themselves why it was that I didn't publicise what was happening to me during the general election of June 1983. Or not tell him that I was pregnant until after he had become Foreign Secretary. What would the consequences have been? Do you really think the Conservative Party would have had a landslide victory in June 1983 if this matter had become public before the election? I and my family did everything we could to avoid a scandal, and my father's correspondence with the Prime Minister was motivated solely by a desire to warn her – to protect her office from what seemed inevitable by that stage.

WOGAN: Do you feel a need to continue to clear your name?

SARA: No I don't. The fact is that even if I ceased to exist, people would still continue to write about me and talk about me. I didn't choose to have this kind of publicity. I would infinitely have preferred not to have had any of it at all. Do you think it has been pleasant? Do you think anybody would wish to have happened to them what happened to me? But if people write about me and say things that are untrue, I cannot let them all pass unchallenged . . .

I really don't understand the idea that a woman's reputation is less important than a man's, or that a woman's career is less important. Why should every single person in this land be entitled to say anything they like about me, my family, my child, but I am supposed to keep quiet?

I think I have as much right as anybody else to express a view about this matter. Or about any other subject under the sun, even political matters. After all, I had embarked on a political career.

Sooner or later, I'll have to try to resume my career. Obviously, that will become necessary. But at the moment I can't do anything in that direction. The career that I had chosen for myself, certainly as far as the Conservative Party is concerned, is barred to me because they have decreed that I am not allowed to be a member of the Conservative Party, I'm not allowed to be a Conservative candidate. They've never given me explanations or justification. There is none of course. So politics seems to be closed for the time being.

WOGAN: What about for another party?

SARA: Well, I certainly won't be supporting the Conservative Party at the next election. Not under the present leadership. I'm very depressed by the trends within the Conservative Party, which seems to me to have become the totalitarian party in Britain, in a sense. The leadership is very intolerant of any other view except that narrow view which is decreed to be the acceptable one of the time.

WOGAN: Your story is as old as time, tragically.

SARA: This is the fundamental mistake that everybody makes. You say the story is as old as time. It's about the eternal triangle – it's about an unfortunate unhappy love affair. It's about adultery, or an illegitimate child. The scandal was not about any of those things. In parliament today there are many people who have been in similar situations and for whom there was no scandal. In fact I think there is a person in the Cabinet who had a child out of wedlock. There is no scandal there.

The scandal, where I was concerned, arose out of the deception of me and my family – and the fact that the Prime Minister, if she didn't actually connive at it, condoned it. From the moment that

93

she knew the facts on polling day 1983, when she apparently was encouraging Cecil Parkinson on a particular course of action – to stay with his wife and family in order to stay with her government – she also knew that I believed that he was going to marry me. And he didn't tell me until September that year.

During that time I suffered the most ghastly experiences at the hands of the press – a car chase across London, the *Daily Mirror* crashing into my car and so on. I think it is unforgivable that she could have been party to that kind of thing happening. I think it was because of the risk of those details becoming public that she decided he had to go.

Patricia Neal

I F ANYONE should deserve an Oscar for bravery, it is
Patricia Neal. She is the living proof that with guts and
determination and being surrounded by loved ones, it is
possible to resume an almost normal life after appalling illness. Patricia was famous once for her 'dark' voice. Her voice
is still dark but with small traces of hesitancy left by multiple
strokes. Not only has she been brave enough to resume her
career, she was brave enough to come and tell me one evening a little of her life story beginning with the three movies she
made with Ronald Reagan.

I was in quite a few films with Ronald Reagan. I was first in *John
Loves Mary* with him. Then I did *The Fountainhead*. Then we went
to England together and we did *The Hasty Heart* here. We lived
side by side in the Savoy. It was very good because I think Jane
Wyman had just announced she was divorcing him. So he and I
practically went steady. Nothing romantic at all. I was in love with
someone else and his love for Jane Wyman was still there. And
then he married Nancy.

He was always interested in politics. I had a friend here in
England, and he would take Ronnie and me out horseriding. He
had us write something once on what we would like to do in our
later lives. It was a jokey kind of thing, and Ronnie wrote 'To be
President of the United States'. I am very pleased to see he made it
and I think he's a very good President. I like him.

The film of mine everyone remembers is *Hud* with Paul Newman. I loved doing that film. I didn't think it was an enormous part

and was surprised to win an Oscar. But when I won one I was very proud. Then I went on to do this great film with John Ford.

We were late in starting the film and before we even started I had this massive stroke. The fact that I am still alive and here today is astonishing. I had three massive strokes in one night followed by an operation. From Hollywood, I was brought back to England.

Roald Dahl, who was my husband, forced me to carry on. He made me practise moving and speaking constantly. You see, having a stroke is really a horrendous thing to happen to one. You have to really work to go on with your life. Roald really wanted me to get back to life the way it should be, the way it was. And he pushed and pushed me. At the time I hated him, I hated everybody, for pushing me. I was a belligerent woman. But I realise now you simply have to not give up, and you have to work very hard. You dare not give up. You must work.

Now, I can say it was worth it – even though I will never be perfect. But I adore life now. It's a beautiful thing that I was allowed to live. And it's thanks to the efforts of everybody around me.

When the worst was over, I went back and made some more movies. I made *The Subject Was Roses*. That was my first film after my stroke. I didn't want to do it at all. On the first day of rehearsal I didn't like it at all. But by the end of the film I was the happiest woman in the world.

Jim Dale

IT WAS a rare pleasure to meet Jim on the first interview he had given in this country for ten years. Well, he was too busy being one of Broadway's biggest stars – a far cry from all those *Carry On* films:

In Britain everyone associates me with the *Carry On* films. But I made my last one about fifteen or twenty years ago. I get little kids stop me in the street, saying 'I saw you last night on television'. And of course in America the *Carry Ons* have become sort of cult films. But only to insomniacs! They are shown at four in the morning. I often meet sleepy-eyed people in the street saying 'Hey man, you're that guy on television'. I don't watch them personally but I have them all on tape.

I think the *Carry Ons* were a marvellous period of English cinema that we captured. It was a great period of English humour. Worthy of the archives. They were knockabout, knickers and all that. Crude, but why not?

I was around even before those films. I was singing even before Cliff Richard. Actually, a long time before Cliff, we were doing the '6 – 5 Special'. Once when they were holding auditions a young boy came along. He had long sideboards, and he sang a song. Dennis Main Wilson, the producer, said to me 'What do you think of him?' I said 'He sounds a lot like Elvis Presley.' He said 'Right son, who are you?' He said 'Cliff Richard.' He said 'Right, thank you, no more. Off you go. Next one, please.' And so poor Cliff was actually sacked before he even got his first job.

I actually started as a stand-up comic and I played at the old Shepherd's Bush Empire. I was on a bill with a wonderful old comedian called Max Miller. The Cheekie Chappie. I did a comedy act as Jim Smith who was just about to join the Royal Air Force, and I thought I'd do something where I'm called up, on the stage. So I had two men dressed as police officers, and they arrested me on stage for not reporting to Padgate. It got a big laugh, me desperately trying to do my act and being marched off. When I actually arrived at Padgate for the real call-up, they were waiting for me! An officer shouted 'Out of all the eighteen hundred new recruits, anybody here with the name Smith?' Of course a hundred stood up. 'Jim Smith?' And ninety-nine sat down. He said 'Yes, come out here, lad. Stand on that table.' I stood on it. He said 'We don't mind you taking the micky out of the RAF. We all do it in our own way, but when you've got the gall to do it in front of three or four million people, that's going a little too far.'

But it was the best thing that could have happened. In those days they needed camp shows every other week, so I spent my time producing them – with maybe a chorus line of boys who had been farmers and coal miners and now they were dressed up in women's costumes doing *La Cage Aux Folles*. Instead of the eight weeks training, I stayed at Padgate for fourteen months.

After the Air Force I made the leap to Shakespeare. My 'Bottom' was the best part. I was doing it with Cleo Laine. She was playing Titania, and we were at the Assembly Rooms at the Edinburgh Festival. I had this wonderful ass's head. I used to come off the stage and had about thirty seconds to put it on and go on stage again. And go 'Eee-aw'!

Frank Dunlop, the director, had a marvellous idea – he thought he would get about twenty-four basset hounds and a hunter to come down the aisle blowing – in the pretty woodland scene with the lovers. On the first night, twenty-four basset hounds came racing down – we'd never seen these dogs before – and they bounded on the stage and sniffed around me. Then they all went off the stage as the hunter blew the horn. A wonderful sight but my ass's head was in the wings. All of them sniffed it, and all of them cocked their legs, and all of them did it. On my ass's head. Not one hound, but twenty-four.

I came off stage. I had twenty seconds. I picked the ass's head up, and it was dripping. I thought, 'What's wrong here?' I put it on, and pow! The stench! The stage manager said 'I've got some powder, love. It'll be all right.' She sprinkled the powder over the head and inside the head too. I put the ass's head on and walked out on to the stage. I didn't speak, I just went 'Achooo!' A cloud of powder came out, about thirty foot long. It brought the house down.

Then I moved to Broadway, eventually to do *Barnum*. When we got the actual script part of *Barnum*, it was just very basic. 'Barnum walks on stage and he climbs up a ladder to visit his wife.' Things like that. I realised there should be more movement in it, and I thought well, here's my chance to do something that could possibly be the most exhausting role ever. (I didn't realise how right I would be!) So I started to suggest things. I knew very well that if I couldn't do it within ten weeks of rehearsal, we could change it and I could walk across and climb up. But if I did do it, it meant I had to do it every night.

The high wire act took me about ten weeks to learn, I suppose. But even on a 34-foot tightrope there comes a time when everybody in the production has had a go on it. Not only the cast – and they can walk it eventually over the months – but the stage hands. I have lingering memories of seeing big American stage hands, walking 34 feet across the tightrope not with ballet shoes but with big boots on! The first thing you learn is how to fall off it, but eventually you can stay on it. You had to be exceedingly fit to do it. Two years of it can knock you out. Ask Michael Crawford.

Michael Crawford

A ND OF course we did. Apart from *Barnum*, Michael
Crawford has made history with his portrayals of Frank
Spencer, *Billy Liar*, and, of course, the *Phantom of the
Opera*. There seems no end to the talents of that brilliant
comedy star and consummate actor. We made history, too,
on the night he came on 'Wogan' – it was the first time I had
devoted an entire show to just one guest:

I was always really very shy. Yet, when I was about six, my
grandmother used to take me to bingo every Monday and Wednesday in Sheerness, and whenever they said 'We want a volunteer to
come and pull the tickets please', I was the first one down the aisle
and on the stage. I stood there and couldn't say a word. I just loved
standing up there and they used to say 'Yes – we had you last week
didn't we?' And I'd say 'Please, let me pull another number.' I
didn't know where I was looking or what I was doing, but I just
liked the feel of it up there.

I was very lucky to have someone who was maybe just an
ordinary lady who was extraordinary and was a great support
through my life. For instance, when I was learning to tap dance for
Billy, which we did at Drury Lane, I spent weeks in the kitchen
during the day and she used to come over and stay with me for
periods of time. She used to sit in the room in the front with a
rosary, saying 45 Hail Marys and 45 Our Fathers for me and she
just said 'How long have you got?' I said 'Another three weeks
now' and she'd say 'I don't think we're going to be ready. I just

don't think I can do it in time.' She almost wore out the rosary beads. I used to tap dance from the cooker, past the sink to the fridge doing sort of step shuffle for three months, and I had to transfer the kitchen work to the Drury Lane stage which was in fact 35 cookers and 25 sinks wide.

She came to see *Billy* and on one occasion she was in the Royal Box. I was playing a scene where my 'mother' comes up to me at this song and – it's fantasy – goes to machine gun me and I say 'Aw, piss off the lot of you!' My grandmother, she stood up in the Royal Box and said 'Michael. I've never heard you use language like that.'

She saw another thing I did where I literally sang *War and Peace* in about three minutes, a great sort of resume of *War and Peace* right down the front of the stage with Cheryl Kennedy, my partner. At the end of it, I had to say to Cheryl 'Did I do good?' and this third face came up from the front of the stage and said 'Darling, you did wonderfully!' I looked round, and there was my grand-mother again.

While I was doing that, I went on a radio thing with Pete Murray where this guy read my handwriting. He said 'Oh, you've got cheeky, bulbous lower loops' and I said 'What does that mean?' He said 'Well, it means you're coyly virile.' So I tried to be polite. I said 'Does this mean I like to turn the lights out?' I went home, and Nan had stayed up. She said 'What happened today?' I said, 'I did the show.' 'I know that. Get to the point. What did he say?' 'He said I was coyly virile.' She said 'What did you say?' I said 'Does that mean I like to turn the light out?' She said, 'Yes, I could never bear to look at it either.' Eight children. You can't blame her really, can you?

The first part which most people remember me for is Frank Spencer in 'Some Mothers Do Have 'Em'. We wanted to include physical stuff to make comedy that would go back to silent days in a way, but have dialogue too, and it's very difficult. Some of those silent characters wouldn't work with dialogue. So you had to find a voice. Now I'd done a play called *No Sex Please, We're British* in which I created this sort of characterisation of a very simple sort of a guy, but extremely honest, so you feel for him, and all the time you wanted to push him and you could understand his frustrations. I took this characterisation and tried it with the Frank Spencer dialogue and I thought we would marry him as well. We had to find someone, I mean, as clever as Michelle Dotrice, to make the marriage believable. Without her, the series wouldn't have worked as well as it did. The character, in a way, is very childlike. I based a lot of it on my younger daughter Lucy. I think all children are very alike. A simple example is if you are sitting having a meal and you say to a child 'Why haven't you eaten your cabbage?' There's a pause which first of all says 'What cabbage?' as if they didn't know cabbage was on the plate. Now, they've established the cabbage is there, and they know that you know the cabbage is there. So then you get 'We both know the cabbage is there' without a word being spoken while they think of an excuse so you will give in to them. It's true. Anyone who has a child or a grandchild will recognise it in all their children. I still do it!

Phineas T. Barnum was a massive change from Frank Spencer. It was a challenge well beyond the realms of what I really wanted to do. I saw the show in New York and thought it was so different. One always wants to put something on a stage that is new and refreshing so that you can get a larger and a more varied kind of audience.

Harold Fielding, our producer, sent me to New York to the Big Apple Circus School to learn the part, and I worked there for about six or seven weeks for about 14 hours a day. It was very demoralising because all the people that work there are between the ages of four and eight, and they do everything. They sort of took me in as a grandfather figure and held my arms and taught me things. I had a Hungarian trainer. I couldn't understand a word he was saying. So whenever he said 'jump', I said 'pardon' and the things went up in the air and my trousers were still on the floor! But eventually I learned to walk the tightrope that was the thickness of the wire and it was 34ft across the stage! I had forgotten how painful the whole show was – and we did twelve hundred-odd shows! To do it eight times a week, it really was quite something. Some mornings, I couldn't get out of bed. I was aching so much that I literally couldn't get out of bed. It took three months for my body to actually recover.

The role of *Phantom of The Opera* is just as exhausting but in a different way. The make-up alone takes about two hours to put on. First of all a skullcap goes on, and then the prosthetics. They are painted and coloured and shaded and then something else goes on to disfigure my nose and eye, my top lip and then the bottom lip, and I am totally unrecognisable.

I don't think anyone has gone to such extravagant lengths for a make-up in a theatre before, but Andrew Lloyd Webber went to an awful lot of trouble writing some rather wonderful music and it's a great character to play. It was worth spending three months creating that make-up.

In fact people come to the show and they don't believe it is me. There's sometimes a few complaints. People have been known in the interval to grab the bar staff and say 'It's a disgrace that we're not told he's not on' and 'Why is he not on' and 'What's that fellow doing out there?' But I am thrilled with the part and of course very honoured to have been awarded the Laurence Olivier award. It made me so happy I cried! I get terribly emotional and spend more time crying when I'm happy than smiling, but I just feel very fortunate and very happy.'

Donald Sinden, Maria Aitken and Roy Hudd

IT WAS an evening of 'Darlings' and 'Sweeties' on 'Wogan' when I asked the actors' actor Donald Sinden to take a seat alongside the producer, director and actress, Maria Aitken, and the man who is keeping music hall and variety alive single handed, Roy Hudd. As one, they raced for the spotlight to compare indiscreet stories about one another and about their profession generally. He doesn't really need it, but cue Donald and have the hook ready . . .

DONALD SINDEN: London happens to be my hobby, knowing my way around London. I haunt an area at the top of St. Martin's Lane, because that's where most people get lost. They come out of Leicester Square Tube station, and they all bring out their maps.

The other day I was there, and two American matrons – they had to be American, blue hair and what-have-you – I thought, wonderful. I dived in there and said 'Can I help?' And they said, 'Yeah, we're trying to find the National Theatre. We thought we'd come down here, through the Trafalgar . . . ' I said, 'No, no, no. Go down here, you come to the Strand, turn left right over Waterloo Bridge, National Theatre, no problem.'

That afternoon I had a matinee at the Duke of York's Theatre. During the matinee a note was sent round to my dressing room and it said 'The two American travellers helped by you this afternoon

failed to recognise you, even though they saw your fine performance in the play last evening. Your kindness to strangers reinforced
our admiration for your artistry, and the British people in general.'
An unsolicited testimonial which I thought rather sweet – except
for the fact that it was addressed to 'Dear Sir John' . . .

MARIA AITKEN: When I first came into the theatre I didn't
know what this expression a 'flat slapper' was. And somebody said
'Oh Donald Sinden is probably the last flat slapper.' What it is is
that when you leave the stage, you hit either the side of the set or
the nearest hard object and that makes the audience clap. In other
words you get your round of applause.

SINDEN: It's sneaky, but yes, of course I do it.

MARIA: Theatre is an extraordinary business. Actually, each
and every first night, you wonder why you do it. Acting is like
adventuring – you have to prepare very carefully against all even-
tualities, and then you do literally step off into the unknown. In the
war, I gather, promiscuity was rife, because you might be bumped
off and you got to know people very well in the air raid shelters
because there was danger. (I don't remember but I have it on very
good authority!) Well my theory is that rehearsing a play is rather
like that. The whole thing could be disastrous. It could be
extremely humiliating, and of course you could be poverty-
stricken at the end of it all. So you become friends with your
colleagues in quite a deep way and quite quickly, because you're
sharing something dangerous.

ROY HUDD: It's a funny thing. Actors and music hall people
were always kind of separate. Actors always used to say 'I'm
playing a theatre', and comics used to say 'I'm working the
theatre'. There is a lovely story of Rob Wilton the great comedian
that illustrates it really. You know, 'The Day War Broke Out' –
well, Rob Wilton was in a pub up north somewhere, and there's an
old actor sitting in the corner. (Perfectly true story, told to me by
Ted Ray.) And this 'Actor' is sobbing quietly at a table by himself.
Rob Wilton went over to him and he said 'Come on, old son, it
can't be as bad as all that. What's the matter? He said, 'I'm – I'm so
lonely.' Rob said 'Come on, cheer yourself up. What would you

like to drink?' He said 'I'll have a triple brandy.' Rob said, 'No wonder you're bloody lonely.'

MARIA: I would have loved to be in variety. I wouldn't mind being Vesta Tilley. I'd like to be in drag. I've always liked those parts. You can do it a bit in Shakespeare if you're 'legit'. Actually I played principal boy once. But in Ireland, in a theatre that was attached to a bar, not the other way round. I hardly ever saw the audience!

SINDEN: So many actors become eccentrics. You find they do the most extraordinary things – like C. Aubrey Smith: before he went on the stage, he always used to say 'Hip-bath, hip-bath, hip-bath'. It made no sense at all. People would be emoting on the stage and the whole audience could hear this 'Hip-bath, hip-bath, hip-bath' backstage.

I love theatrical anecdotes. In fact I collect them. One of my favourites is about Maria. I am sure she remembers. Years ago in a play, she had a small part where the hero was supposed to fire a gun, and somebody on the other side of the stage threw on a partridge. So, as he fired the gun a partridge would fall down. Maria was on the stage, and it came to this moment when the hero fired his gun and nothing happened. So he cleverly fired the other barrel. Wham! And with great presence of mind – with no partridge appearing – Maria collapsed dying on the stage. At the same moment somebody else threw the partridge on. Wonderful!

MARIA: It taught me something about the nature of comedy. It's no joke when two things die from the barrel of a gun!

HUDD: It's an old adage, isn't it? 'Timing is the thing'. What's the secret of comedy? 'Timing', they always say. But I don't think there's any secret in timing. It's just "don't talk when the audience are laughing".That's the basic secret.

One of the first pantomimes I did was with a northern comic and he played dame. I was feeding him, being straight man to him, and he cracked some gag. It got a big laugh and I came in with the next line right on top of the laugh. I knew I'd done wrong. I came off and as he followed me off, I said 'I'm terribly sorry' and he went bang! and hit me straight in the mouth. He said 'You won't do it again, will you, son?' One way of learning timing! The gentle art of theatre.

SINDEN: That reminds me about Macready, when he was playing *Macbeth*, (and I'm keeping my fingers crossed). There came a time when he had to come on to the stage holding the daggers with his hands covered in blood. His dresser always waited in the wings for him with a bowl of theatrical blood. He used to dip his hands in there, pick up the daggers and go back on again. One night he came off and the dresser wasn't there. He looked quickly for him and there was nobody. But there was a complete stranger standing there in the wings. Macready went over to him, punched him on the nose and he got his blood!

Ears were burning all over the West End of London that night as we chatted on in hostility. Donald is lucky to be in this book at all; in each of the three times he has appeared on 'Wogan' he promises me I'll be in the next volume of his memoirs – so far nothing!

Jonathan Miller

S OME PEOPLE dress up to come on Wogan – some like
  Zsa Zsa Gabor spectacularly so. But there are certain
people who you would not recognise if they did not look the
way they always have – a certain distinguished seediness, if
you see what I mean.

Jonathan Miller is one of them. One of the great story-
tellers of the age, yet no natty dresser. His shoes, on the day I
met him, looked like a kind of superannuated wellington
boot. Apparently, they were the height of fashion and he had
bought them by post from a firm in Newport in the USA. This
great director of theatre and opera (although he can't read
music) let me in on some of the family history and his own
private thoughts . . .

My grandparents came to this country from Lithuania in about
1870. My father's family settled in the East End of London, and my
mother's father came from Lithuania at the age of twelve, I think in
about 1870. He was despatched by his parents, on his own, with
nothing but a violin. He was despatched to New York. But the boat
stopped in Ireland *en route* and he got off at Cork, believing it was
New York. As he didn't speak any English at all, he didn't discover
the mistake until about ten years later. In fact he flourished. He
started as a pedlar, and he became quite a prosperous gent.

When I was very young, it was my ambition to be a doctor. I had
no idea of being in the theatre at all. In fact, I have always wished

that I had continued in medicine. I wish I had been a better mathematician. I don't think medicine is more worthwhile. I just think I had the chance of being quite good at it. Also there's a sort of faint feeling when you're doing something like science that there's a permanent record which is always there. The sad thing about the theatre, which is also an exhilarating thing about the theatre, is that there's a sort of excitement about it at the moment you're doing it, and then there's no trace at all except in the memories of those who hopefully enjoyed the production which you made.

A medical training has turned out to be quite useful in the theatre – to look, to observe, to notice what people do. It makes you impatient with the sort of cliches which usually happen in the theatre. I was doing a workshop with some students in the United States a while ago and I was doing a scene from *The Marriage of Figaro*. There's a scene where the countess has to faint on seeing Susannah come out of the closet, and the girl actress in fainting clapped her hands to her forehead.

Now, that is a cliche which only exists in the theatre. People who are fainting never clap their hands to their forehead. I asked her 'Where did you see that?' And she was nonplussed – she couldn't say where she'd seen it. Of course the only place she had ever seen it was on the stage. A medical training makes you focus your attention on what people do, how they act, the tiny nuances of behaviour, upon which diagnosis depends if you're a doctor, and upon which really the success of a play depends if you're a director.

I only got into theatre, you know, because I was good at imitating chickens. In fact, whenever I got written about, when I was on the stage, in those early days, I was described as one sort of animal after another. There was a demented camel, or a curious horse, or some such. Simply because I'm ungainly. And I have a long nose.

From those days, some of my happiest memories on the stage are, of course, from *Beyond The Fringe*. Who would have guessed then that the various members would develop as they have? I think we are all rather surprised about what's happened to us. We would never have guessed it at the time. You'd never have guessed Dudley Moore was going to be a sex symbol. However, he was pursued by very attractive young ladies from the very word go. All throughout the performances of *Beyond The Fringe*, extremely

109

attractive young women were going up the stairs to his dressing room. And he would sometimes come late on to the stage.

Beyond The Fringe was, I think, probably the first time a group of young men had gone on to the stage who did not come from showbiz – who had a university education. For that reason we had interests which were slightly wider than the traditional showbiz interests, so that we were bound to apply ourselves to all sorts of things which were of interest, like politics. From that grew the idea that a new wave of hard-hitting satire had been born, although I must say that satire was one of those things which was invented largely by the press. Actually it wasn't very hard-hitting. It was amusing. I don't think there was anything really vicious or subversive about what we did. In fact we were often told how extremely much members of the establishment we were already. Certainly, I don't think we threatened anything at all. But I think we started something. I think the sort of programme you have now, like *The Young Ones*, couldn't have happened unless we had made this rather sensitive little break in the dyke very early on . . .

The only person who figured in *Beyond The Fringe* by name really was Harold Macmillan, and it was a very famous impersonation that Peter Cook did. (I think he loved doing it because he rather liked being him.) He once did it on the stage with Harold Macmillan there in the audience! We stood in the wings breathless with anticipation, watching what Peter was going to do. He has a sort of kamikaze instinct for doing the worst possible thing when something like that happens.

So there was Macmillan sitting on the eighth row, and Peter was doing his imitation. He said 'A lot of people write to me and ask, and say what do you do when you hear that a group of young men are impersonating you down at the Fortune Theatre? I reply, I go down to the theatre and sit there in the eighth row with a fatuous grin all over my face and pretend it's not happening.' And of course the audience turned round and applauded Harold Macmillan!

Unfortunately, there's a great deal more to complain about nowadays. I think the situation in society is much more vicious. One of the great things about England is that it has, year by year, absorbed all sorts of people from everywhere and made them into English men and women. I feel that there is some sort of reduction

110

in that hospitality in recent years. I think England has become noticeably a more racist country than it was. Although there has always been a very special and peculiar sort of hostility felt towards Jews, for all sorts of complicated reasons, none of which are justified, nevertheless it's possible and much easier for Jews to pass for Englishmen in the end and eventually to become Englishmen. It's much harder for people from India and Africa and the Caribbean to become recognisably English because they are still noticeably of a different colour. I think it's very regrettable that our hospitality in this country towards those people is less accommodating in recent years than it has been to people of my race.

HRH
Princess Michael

OF ALL members of the Royal Family, the one who sticks in the craw of the tabloids is Princess Michael of Kent. Perhaps because she's a foreigner (how many generations are the Royal Family themselves removed from Germany?) Or is she really as 'pushy', outspoken and indiscreet as the press portray her? When we spoke together, she was in the midst of another flailing, over supposed plagiarism, in her book *Crowned In A Far Country*. It seemed as good a place as any to start:

PRINCESS MICHAEL: It's unfortunate really that I didn't put quotes on one or two little bits. I forgot to do that. It was an oversight. I'm afraid I was rather distracted at the time I was doing that particular bit. I had a few other things to think about. But – and this is something nobody's bothered to point out – I've credited everyone at the end of the book. They're all mentioned, everybody whose research work I've used.

WOGAN: It seems unfortunate that the press will always find something to knock you about.

PRINCESS M: Oh well, I suppose, princesses are fair game in Fleet Street. It's for me to rise above. I have a very organised staff who won't let me read anything, so I'm usually the last to know. Sometimes I feel I should know. Then they tell me.

WOGAN: How do you react when you read something manifestly untrue about yourself?

PRINCESS M: It used to be worse. But now I sort of just shrug my shoulders. I have tremendous faith in the good sense of the British public, you know. They're very good to me, and I don't think they believe half of it either.

WOGAN: Do stress and tension play a large part in your life?

PRINCESS M: Yes. Yes. I always appear outwardly calm, and inside it's churning. I think most people in the public eye have a lot of stress and tension. You must do, Terry. I saw you pacing up and down outside, chewing your fingernails.

WOGAN: That was me, yes. It's a bad habit. But you are restricted in the kind of reactions or how you can reply. The frustration must build up a good deal. Sometimes you must feel like striking out.

PRINCESS M: Well, I think you have to deal with it in your own way. I go home to the country and I fiddle around in my garden which I love and I am with my animals and my children, and try very much not to pay any attention.

WOGAN: Are you as calm at home as you are outwardly, or do you take it out on the cat?

PRINCESS M: Never the cats, no! Cats are very special. Do you know, Queen Victoria had cats, and her eldest daughter Vicky, who became the Empress Frederick and the mother of Kaiser Bill, she wrote to her mother every day and sometimes about cats. One very pathetic letter springs to mind. She wrote saying she had just been for a walk in the garden and she'd seen her favourite cat nailed to a tree with its nose cut off. And she'd admonished her son that he should do something about it, and asked who would do such a thing. And the son said 'Well, that's perfectly all right with me because the cats eat the birds, and I want to shoot the birds and I don't want to feed the cats.' So she wrote to her mother to ask what should she do. Queen Victoria said 'Well I put a little silver collar with V.R. on it around the neck of all my cats so that when they're out in the garden the keepers see the glint of the collar and they don't shoot *my* cats.' It was cats in those days instead of corgis.

WOGAN: I can't imagine anyone having a pot-shot at a corgi.

113

You have just returned from America. What do they make of you there. How do they address you?

PRINCESS M: Oh dear, yes. That can become quite amusing really. Sometimes it happens when I'm with a group of people who don't know. If we've had dinner together and we've had a bit of wine at dinner and they've relaxed a little bit, and loosened their collars, they pluck up the courage and drop the 'Princess' and call me Michael.

WOGAN: And probably even 'Hi Mike' – is it as bad as that?

PRINCESS M: No, but I'm sure we'll get there.

WOGAN: Do you think the Royal family will ever suffer from over-exposure? That if we see too much of them we'll get tired of them?

PRINCESS M: I don't know. I think it's a double-edged sword, isn't it, because on the one hand there's obviously the demand, otherwise there wouldn't be so many books and magazines featuring us if people didn't want to see us. It's not always pleasant for us.

WOGAN: Would it be better if you held yourself a bit more aloof?

PRINCESS M: Well, that's how it used to be, wasn't it? And then this new wave came in of seeing us as real people.

WOGAN: And you're not, of course.

PRINCESS M: Of course not, no. We're all made of latex like on *Spitting Image*.

WOGAN: Your book *Crowned in a Far Country* – did you write it for profit?

PRINCESS M: Aha! Partly, but I didn't know it was going to sell. That's just the next step. I wanted a new career . . .

WOGAN: Did you need the money?

PRINCESS M: Everybody needs money. We don't have a Civil List, and so we have to earn our living. This is part of my little contribution. I'm going to keep the proceeds, which other members of the family can't, you see.

WOGAN: It's hard for the public to imagine that Princess Michael of Kent would need money, in writing a book.

PRINCESS M: Do you think they want to see me doing my own hair, washing up? No, I want this to be a career, I want to write. I've always wanted to do it, and I think you shouldn't leave things left undone that you wanted to do.

WOGAN: You're going to write some more?

PRINCESS M: Yes. I've mastered my word processor now.

Telly Savalas

EVERY YEAR Telly Savalas comes over to England to play golf, and to play it well. For the past two years he's carried off the Celebrity Prize at the Wang Four-Stars Pro-Am at Moor Park. He plays the game as he does the game of life – relaxedly, good-humouredly, self-deprecatingly. And with a cigar rather than a lollipop. He's one of those guests on 'Wogan' who can entertain just by being there. He keeps telling me that he is going to settle down to a respectable middle-aged life, but so far I see no signs. On one of his visits he told me not only about his early acting days but about his American-Greek family:

I come from a well-off family, I come from a destitute family, and I come from a middle-and-between family. Pop was the kind of guy that took us up and down the scales. Whatever it was, there was consistency to his personality, which made it all very exciting. You name it, he did it.

My Mom is one of the most outstanding and beautiful women of the world. It's a strange thing. When you've got your Mom like I have, you're still a little kid, you know? 'Telly', she says 'you're not taking care of yourself.' And 'Telly, it's snowing outside, put on your boots.' But as soon as you lose your Mom, you become the older generation. So, I've still got my Mom and I'm still a kid. Not even approaching middle-age.

My uncle was a shrink, and was a total nut. He used to treat patients in our house. You know, the lowest scale of schizophrenia, and he'd take these patients. He left them in the family house one night, and he disappears and shows up two months later. And don't you know, those patients were cured just by staying in our house.

As a kid I grew up on the streets of New York, American-born, but Greek. But you must understand something. I'm not responsible for what the press writes about my ambiguity and being diffuse about certain questions. For the most part, what I say is true. Except, don't believe it, because I might change my mind.

As a grown-up actor, I owe the biggest break in my life to Burt Lancaster. I happened to do this television show for a gag, and Burt saw it. He thought 'This guy might be good for my picture', which was *The Bird Man of Alcatraz*. And don't you know, I go out to Hollywood, California to be in the picture with Burt, and I'd be damned – I got an Academy Award nomination.

Everyone remembers my bald head. If I let my hair grow, I don't think I'd ever work again. I came into life bald and I'm going to go out the same way.

I originally shaved my head for a picture called *The Greatest Story Ever Told*. George Stevens, the great director – he made so many wonderful pictures – he says 'Mr. Savalas, you are going to play Pontius Pilate. He's not effeminate. This man is a powerful general. It would give a feeling of power if I could shave your head. How do you feel about that?' I said 'I don't care, if the price is right. But I got little kids at home, you know, and I don't want them to be traumatised when they see their Pop without any hair.' He said 'Well, bring them in.' I said 'But you're ready to shoot.' He said 'We'll cancel production. We'll shoot the next day.'

And sure enough that's what he does at the cost of 60,000 dollars, or whatever. I bring the kids in the next day to watch me get my head shaved. Don't you know, they never even noticed! And it's been that way ever since.

It was a great picture. When I got the part, the first thing I did was call home. 'Mom, I'm going to be in *The Greatest Story Ever Told*.' She said 'That's wonderful, Telly, you'll be a great Jesus.' I said 'No Mom, I'm playing Pontius Pilate.' She said 'Be sympathetic.' So, without changing history, that's what I did.

117

Sir David Attenborough

O NE OF the first guests on the show and a man full of
anecdotes of all manner of life on earth . . .

I used to do three programmes a week. In those early days, most of
it was live, just like 'Wogan'. But on a lot of occasions, I was
dealing with animals rather than people. Sometimes the animals
are an improvement on the people. But sometimes they give
enormous trouble.

We once had a little flying squirrel (I should explain that we only
had two studios in those days in Alexandra Palace, and so each
studio was on every night, and maybe two or three times a night).
We did an animal programme in the early evening, and we had this
little flying squirrel. The flying squirrel stood on the table, and it
saw the microphone boom and it went ooof, like that, and it was
gone! The interesting thing was, you see, that everybody knew that
it was loose in the studio. So 'Watch the epilogue tonight, boys'
because he was going to be there. And he was. There was the
cleric, and over his shoulder this little flying squirrel. It lived in the
studio for a week. He appeared in plays, in documentaries . . .
They were good moments.

I occasionally interviewed people. I had to interview a very
famous zoologist who was an expert in animal language. He had
written a book called *King Solomon's Ring*, in about 1955 or 1956.
So I was sitting (just as one does, on 'Wogan'). I said, 'Now,
Professor, I understand you can actually speak to the animals.'
And he said 'Ja, that is so.' I said 'And you are particularly fluent in

Greylag Goose language.' And he said 'Ja, ja.' So I said 'As it happens we have a Greylag Goose here and I wonder if you would have a few words with it.'

So we brought this goose on and put him on the table. We'd brought it from the London Zoo, and as it was the middle of the night it was a little upset. He started flapping his wings. The Professor said 'Ah, mein liebchen, no no no, komm, komm, komm.' And he took hold of it and as he did so, he said 'Have a few words with me.' And the goose went pwwwwt! 'Oh dear, dear, all over ze trousers!'he said. He was so embarrassed . . . It was all live!

Thankfully, I have never been seriously attacked by an animal, but I've had a few worrying moments. You remember Elsa the lioness? Well, I was on my way to Madagascar and we got a message saying could we call in on this lioness. So we got a small plane, landed in Nairobi, chartered another plane and went out to this place where Joy Adamson was. When we arrived Joy said 'Oh, disaster! Elsa's sick. She has disappeared.'

I was worn out, so I got a camp bed and I went to sleep down by the river. I woke up with a terrible weight on me, and this appalling halitosis. Elsa was actually lying on me and her saliva was dribbling. I thought, what do I do? What do I do? I didn't do anything really except lie there, and then Elsa got up and stretched and went away!

The nice thing about animals is they are not trying to sell themselves. They're not trying to preach messages. They're not politicians. They're not arguing. They're not putting on acts. They are unfailingly surprising. They're marvellously beautiful – what more do you want?

Few people would believe the time it takes to film some animals. In 'Life on Earth', we wanted a shot of a strange little frog which actually incubates its tadpoles in its throat – the male frog does this. But nobody had ever seen one being, as it were, 'born'. This frog lived in Tierra del Fuego at the southern tip of South America, and we caught some of these pregnant male frogs. We looked at them, and they looked at us, but nothing happened.

We put them in a tobacco tin and took them back to Bristol to a chap called Rodger Jackman, a great naturalist cameraman – and he took these, he looked at them, they looked at him. Rodger made a little set for them, and they looked at one another, and nothing happened. Rodger went to bed and in the morning there was the male frog looking proud, you see. With a little baby alongside.

So Rodger and his assistant between them watched the remaining pregnant male frogs day and night, never taking their eyes off them, because if they did a frog would go 'cough' and that would be that. After about 150 hours of watching a frog sort of gave him a slightly cross-eyed look, and Rodger, with this mystic skill which cameramen have, pressed the button, the camera whirled, the frog went 'cough', a little baby shot out of its mouth, and that was on film!

People sometimes complain that there's too much sex in wildlife films, but it's very fascinating. Take spiders. Certain male spiders give their mates a little present. They actually catch a little morsel. They wrap it up in silk, and they give it to this large fat lady who is their wife, and say 'What do you think of that?' And while she is unwrapping it just to see what this present is, the male spider nips around the back and gets on with things.

And scorpions. The gentleman scorpion just leaves a little packet on the ground, and gets hold of the female by the claws and says, 'Come this way, dear' and dances, and finally when it's just in the right position, bingo! I think that's very romantic.

Anne Bancroft

E VERY NOW and again an interview stays in my mind as
an epic piece of television – but for quite the wrong
reason. It seemed to me by the reaction the next day, that
every single person in the country watched, almost too scared
to breathe, as British Academy Award winner, winner of two
Tony Awards and an Oscar, wife of Mel Brooks and star of
The Graduate, Anne Bancroft nervously picked her way
across the stage to what must have seemed to her the ogre
who was going to grill her.

The conversation was for much of the time monosyllabic. I
began by asking Anne about her meeting with Royalty at her
film premiere the night before. The conversation, if that is the
right word, went something like this:

WOGAN: Did you get to exchange words with any members of
Royalty?

ANNE BANCROFT: I did.

WOGAN: You didn't speak until you were spoken to, I hope?

ANNE: I don't remember. Are you not supposed to?

WOGAN: No, you're not supposed to. I had the pleasure of
interviewing your husband Mel Brooks, about four years ago. He
told me that I had to talk to you.

ANNE: Why?

WOGAN: Because he said you do most of the stuff for him, you write most of the gags. He said you're his inspiration.

ANNE: Oh that's not true.

WOGAN: Is he your inspiration? Is he a help to you?

ANNE: No. We barely see each other, to tell you the truth.

WOGAN: That's not good, is it?

ANNE: Well, it is, yes. At times it's good.

WOGAN: In your new film, *84 Charing Cross Road*, you swap letters with Anthony Hopkins, but you don't meet him. He is in London and you are in New York. You acted separately. That can't have been easy. How did you do that?

ANNE: What do you mean, how?

WOGAN: Well, it must be quite difficult to generate a character.

ANNE: Well, it's a lot easier than this.

WOGAN: You don't find this easy?

ANNE: No, I don't find this easy at all.

WOGAN: Didn't Mel Brooks give you the book as a birthday present, or anniversary?

ANNE: Oh no, that's a pack of lies.

WOGAN: Why do you hate this kind of interviewing so much? Is it me?

ANNE: Probably.

WOGAN: Do you do any of this stuff in America?

ANNE: No.

WOGAN: Are you glad to do this one?

ANNE: No.

WOGAN: It's nearly the end of the show. Thank you, Anne Bancroft.

Robert Morley

I T TOOK a long time for Robert Morley to come on the 'Wogan' show. Well, he is always so busy. But I'm ashamed to say that it was misplaced rumours that he was dying in hospital that made us urgently request a visit. Thankfully, it was only a rumour; he was as fit and well and rotund as ever. At 78, he had all the signs that he would live to be as old as Methuselah. After sampling the sumptuous fare laid out for his delectation in 'hostility', it was difficult to drag him down the narrow stairs and on to the stage – but we managed even though he dropped his plate of Côte de Veau Normande and Confit d'Oie en route.

The conversation was up to the usual Morley wicked sense of fun. I was never sure whether I was interviewing him or he was interviewing me!

You must always die at the right moment, you know. For your obituary. It's important not to have it clashing with someone important. My epitaph is going to be 'Here lies the simple man who tried to do the work of ten. Had there been nine others he might have succeeded. So here to greatness let him lie.' Yes, there were rumours that I was supposed to have gone. One evening, a journalist rang up from somewhere and said 'Is it true? How are you feeling?' He said 'Half the press is at the Westminster Hospital. Robert Morley is supposed to be there and quite ill.' Of course that did worry me. But what I wanted to know was what happened to the other half of the press? Where were *they*?

I've enjoyed life. I've had a wonderfully happy life. People have been kind to me. I've been immensely kind to them. I don't care what I eat, I am not ever worried about keeping slim. I'm a perfect shape. Everyone now is too thin. Sometimes they're even fatter than me. But it's a great mistake to imagine that everyone should be a sylph-like character. When I was made, God said 'Let's make a good one' or something like that. It's so sad when the trolley goes past untouched. I've taught all my children to say 'When the sweet trolley comes, I'll have a little of that' and then when the man fills the plate they say 'Oh, and I might have that too'. So they get two sweets for the price of one. It's very sensible. You should try it some time.

I am not planning on retirement. I have a new chicken commercial in America so I'm planning on an entirely new sort of come-back. A renaissance. I used to sell tinned soup in Australia. But I lost that contract – to Penelope Keith. I try and smile whenever I see her. There's a certain amount of jealousy, you know.

I'm not a great supporter of the old capitalist system – I'm a convinced socialist. You know, we're waiting to get back. It's easier than *being* back, I should think – in the present climate of this country. I'm very left. At least I pay 10/6 a year. One can't do more. A man comes to collect it at the door. Of course, my great bloomer, in the last election but one, was when the press asked me my opinion. Can you imagine this same attractive, intelligent Robert Morley opined that it would be 'a great mistake having a lady Prime Minister because if there was a crisis she'd lock herself in the lavatory'. That was the silliest thing said by anyone that year.

It's a great honour to come on your programme. I watch you every evening. Except, Wednesday when they have 'This Is Your Life'. Who can resist Eamonn Andrews? Hiding in that corridor wearing a porter's cap. Something they don't have anywhere else. And like you, Terry, he's a survivor.

Glenys Kinnock

NOW THE one woman who has been accused by the Tory press of not only pushing her man, but moulding him. Which of course the lady firmly denies. She's undeniably a woman of strongly-held opinions and beliefs and she's not afraid to voice them.

This conversation was before the last election when some were said to believe she was running the Labour Party.

I don't influence Neil. We've got a very close relationship, but he's leader of the Labour Party, and the suggestion that I would in any way wish to lead the Labour Party *through* him is ridiculous. No more than he would want to advise me on how I ought to teach seven-year-olds to read.

He listens to me. He respects my opinion but that's really the basis of any marriage. We do have many opinions in common. But as far as actually running the Labour Party, which is a suggestion which Norman Tebbitt and Edwina Currie were trying to make, that's ridiculous. Nothing is further from the truth.

This is the first kind of attack that has been levelled directly at me. But it was very short-lived. I treated it with the contempt I thought it deserved. I very quickly said that it is ridiculous to suggest that you haven't got a right to express a political opinion unless you're an elected representative. I'm a citizen as much as anyone else, and if I had strongly-held views then I think I have a right to express them. I'm a very political person. Have been since I was in my pram almost.

I am very supportive of Neil. We are very close. It isn't a case of one dominating the other. It's not necessary to be like that. I'm a teacher, first and foremost, that's what I am. Like most women, I balance roles of teaching and being a mother and one or two other things. Mostly my life is a very mundane one.

I don't relish all the attention I receive. But most of the time my life is very ordinary. I don't always go on the 'Wogan' show. I'm not always in glamorous situations. I'm in my jeans and at school teaching, or making packed lunches, or washing football kits. Mine's not the glamorous life at all.

Sir Robin Day

L AST TIME Robin Day appeared on the show, I called in to 'hostility' at five to seven to find him asleep over a plate of our renowned Mousse de Foie Gras en Brioche! Not surprising really, since he had just finished his marathon stint covering the General Election. He was understandably light-headed, having had only three hours sleep, and being woken accidentally by having the voice of Frank Bough on 'Break-fast Time' fed into his dressing room! But on stage, in the heat of the lights, Robin responded like an old trouper to the audience in the TV theatre. He loves to please them – he should really have been an actor.

He began in his usual polite way:

SIR ROBIN DAY: It's very nice of you to invite me. I didn't realise your programme was still going on. Congratulations.

WOGAN: You were talking to the Prime Minister this after-noon about her new cabinet. She gave you short shrift a bit, didn't she? 'Don't try that one on,' she said.

SIR ROBIN: No. She didn't use that phrase.

WOGAN: What phrase did she use? You've forgotten, haven't you?

SIR ROBIN: No. I remember every word in detail. She said 'Ask me any names you like, you'll get the same answer.' But she said she'd be twanging her harp in heaven when I said she might carry on being Prime Minister till the year 2000. I wanted to keep it humorous you see, because we hadn't had much humour in the election. Did you vote, by the way?

WOGAN: I did. I exercised my franchise.

SIR ROBIN: You have a vote in this country?

WOGAN: Certainly. You've been very kind to aliens over the years. And don't think we're not appreciative of it.

SIR ROBIN: I must make a note of that, and write to my MP and get it stopped.

WOGAN: Who is your MP?

SIR ROBIN: I've forgotten.

WOGAN: Do you think after the many years you've been taxing the politicians with keen questions . . .

SIR ROBIN: They've been taxing me.

WOGAN: But really, you did revolutionise – I don't wish to be sycophantic – political interviewing. Have they got wise to you now? Do they adopt a different attitude from the past?

SIR ROBIN: Yes. If the big television interview – the one lasting an hour – if it was ever a serious branch of television journalism or democratic communication or an art form, which is doubtful, but if it ever was, it isn't any longer. It's finished. It's dead. Politicians don't engage in dialogue any more. They just say what they want to say. You ask your questions and they say what they want to say. You might as well be talking in another language. They say what their advisers have told them to say, and an interviewer might as well on most occasions say 'Mr. or Mrs. So-and-So, what is your answer to my first question?' and come back 45 minutes later.

WOGAN: You're known for interrupting –

SIR ROBIN: No, I'm not. I'm not. I'm not. If you look at the transcripts of my interviews recently, you'll find I hardly interrupt. If you interrupt in the middle of a sentence it shows you haven't listened to what they're saying. That's obviously rude. It's rude in any conversation. But if they've ended a sentence once, twice, three, four, five times – and I can think of at least two politicians who have a gift of continuing their sentence at least seventeen times before they come to the end so that you can't get in – it's very difficult.

WOGAN: Which of the leaders you have interviewed impressed you most? Can you say that?

SIR ROBIN: Well, I'm not trying to evade the answer, but that isn't a question which I've ever really asked myself until you've asked me to think about it. I say to myself, now what do I have to ask them? And how David Steel for instance answers his questions, or David Owen, you judge that in a different way from Margaret Thatcher, because she is the Prime Minister. During the election, David Steel and David Owen impressed me greatly because they obviously weren't doing very well and they spoke out with tremendous guts and show of optimism, and they put on a good 'Two Ronnies' show which didn't in fact come off all that well. But they had bags of guts and spirit.

I'm impressed with Kinnock because he had a great deal of fire and eloquence. The fact that I couldn't get a word in edgeways didn't alter the fact that I was quite impressed with him. He put himself across well. A lot of people, even though they didn't follow what he was saying, were impressed with his flow of sincere language. And I was impressed with the Prime Minister because she does have real passion and ferocity about those things she feels strongly about, and you can't deny that to her.

WOGAN: Is this really your last election? Rumour has it that you won't front another election.

SIR ROBIN: I don't know what you mean by fronting. I have always told you, Terry, I just have a humble walking-on part. I think probably at the next election I shall be in a retirement home in somewhere like Eastbourne and I'll be one of the callers to Election Call.

Cyril Smith

ONE OF the most remarkable, and in more ways than one, outstanding figures in recent years on the British political scene is the Liberal MP for Rochdale – a man who on his appearance in the first few weeks of 'Wogan' proved that his personality and opinion more than matched his size. His imminent appearance caused consternation to the Wogan team – a special chair had to be made which is still used to this day for persons of outstanding size. It's still called the Cyril Smith memorial chair. Together, on screen, he helped slim me down a treat. So, naturally enough, we began by first discussing his 29 stones.

Far from having any regrets, he saw his size as a positive advantage and said it was one of the reasons he had been asked to appear on the show!

Being my size means you are different from other people, and in a political sense that is worth something. It means I'm not just one of those old stodgy-type politicians. If you stand on a platform, people will look up at you, look and listen. And if you walk down the street people know you, and who you are. So it does have its distinct advantages.

It may surprise you to know that as a child I actually went to a school for delicate children for twelve months. But these days I don't know how I would feel if I was slim. But I'm not worried. My weight doesn't bother me. I'm perfectly happy to be 29 stones, even though I can't see my shoes when I'm cleaning them!

When I was a child, times were very hard indeed. I don't say there's nobody that's experienced as much poverty as I have, but there's certainly nobody who has experienced more. But we managed. We kept a full table, and a good table. You didn't get butter on the bread, you got dripping on the bread.

When I left school I actually went into the civil service and I was sacked for taking part in politics. After that I went to work in a wages office, then I was a party political agent, then I had my own newsagent's business. Then I started my own business in 1963. My one political ambition then was to be Mayor of Rochdale. I never had any ambition to be a Member of Parliament.

Quite frankly, being an MP has been a great disappointment. I'm not happy in the House of Commons, I'm not happy making speeches in the House of Commons. I find a great deal of hypocrisy there. I find a great deal of repetition of speeches for the sake of it. You can actually see the Whips going round pleading with MPs to speak in order to keep a debate going till ten o'clock, because the vote's at ten o'clock and there's nobody there and they've got to get them all there for the vote.

Maybe it was naive of me to imagine that it was going to be anything different. Perhaps I ought to have known better, but I prefer to think that it was just lack of experience.

I joined the party that was right for me – the Liberals. In fact it is the only party that could contain me. If I'd been in either the Labour Party or the Tory Party, I would have been expelled. I chose not to stand as an Independent. If you talk to people in this country, they all say 'Oh we don't like politics in local government' or 'We don't like politics in national government. We want the best men', and all this. But the fact is that the people of this country vote political leaders and there are very few of us, very few, that beat the system. That is a fact.

I originally won Rochdale not because I was nationally known but because I was locally known. This sounds big-headed – but it matches the body! I probably would get more votes as an Independent in Rochdale than any other Independent. But I still don't think I'd win the seat. I'd do very well, but I don't think I'd win. I need the Liberal vote, which is about 10,000 votes in Rochdale, together with the 10,000 I can put to it on a personal basis.

I believe the best advice I gave the Liberal Party was that in my view the SDP should have been strangled at birth. That's not out of disrespect to the SDP. I have great regard for David Owen and for his abilities. It is simply that I took the view that three parties vying for the popular vote in this country was enough, and if two parties were contesting for the same third-party vote, then all you were going to do was divide the votes and the net result would be that none of you won. I am not sure whether or not the Alliance will grow. If it doesn't grow at the next election, it's going to be a very long time. I think it will grow at the next election, but by then I will have had enough. This is the last parliament in which I shall serve, certainly as a Member of Parliament.

It has always been my intention to retire at 60 anyway. When you're dragging 29 stone and you're approaching 60, and you're going down to London on the train, and you're going back to Rochdale – when you're doing that two and three times a week, it's a hell of a job. I just want to be able to do it when I want to do it, rather than when I have to do it.

I consider I've given the Liberal Party much more than it's given me. I think there are Liberal MPs in the House of Commons today who would not be in the House of Commons if I had not won Rochdale in 1972, so I think I've made my contribution.

But as we all know, it was not the end for Big Cyril – the 1987 General Election saw him elected again for Rochdale on his personal vote.

After the show, like the dutiful MP he is, he took one of the programme's fleet of turbo cars and headed for Euston Station for the rush back North – he didn't even wait for a doggy bag with a little duck with sauerkraut and apple stuffing and 'hostility's' famour Poires Belle Dijonaise – he couldn't get back to the dripping butties quickly enough . . .

132

Luciano Pavarotti

A S IF he wasn't big enough, in every sense of the word, Luciano Pavarotti insisted on his own chair. Well, large stool really, for I found myself conducting this conversation from a position some two feet below the great man. It is rarely that one gets the opportunity to look right up the left nostril of one of the world's great singers. But enough of the nose, what was so special about the Pavarotti vocal cords?

I don't think a voice is special. I think it is special in the way you produce the voice and put everything together. It's not just the voice, not just the sound. If you go by the sound, there are many other sounds and they are better than mine. I say that without trying to be modest. I really think so. These sounds that are better than mine, they belong to singers that I know. They are not first-rate singers. But the voices are better. So I think it is more in the way you use the voice, the power which you have to use it during the entire aria, to finish the aria well. (When I say aria, I use the word to make everybody understand, but I should say opera.) I am always convinced of what I am doing, even if sometimes I'm a little bit out here and there, like anybody. I'm always convinced of what I'm doing.

You may have noticed I hold a handkerchief at recitals. The handkerchief began when I began recitals in 1973. Can you imagine a tenor going in front of people without a set? He doesn't know what to do with the hands. So I tried it in front of the mirror, many positions, and I did not like any of them. Then I took the handkerchief in one hand. And I began like that, and the expression on the face became very good. And after a while I was more and more relaxed, until now I think it is my partner. I cannot stay without it.

I do some concerts in big arenas when I do not have time to go in a place like London to make several performances in the theatre. I come here to share with several thousand people beautiful moments of music. It makes me happy and I hope it will make them happy. In these places, I think there is another kind of audience that we did not reach before. It is for the good of the opera. I think that is good, makes the opera a little more known. I am very keen on popularising the opera. It's what I try to do.

Some say opera is old-fashioned, an antique thing like furniture, not like modern furniture made now. Composers do not write now for voices like mine. It's not that they don't write beautiful music, don't misunderstand me. But yes, opera is old-fashioned, like a *bel canto* opera. But in the way it is made today, I think it can be very modern. The stage director lately has invaded the world of the opera positively and has given the world of the opera very important things.

You say, which production are you doing, are you doing a new production? But that is good. That is the positive part. It makes the world of the opera very popular. I want everybody to go to it. More than buffs, the privileged people in the past who had the money to go. Now everybody should go. The instrument to make opera popular is the television. I think if you put a performance on the television, then it becomes popular. So you say 'I won't pay £100 to go to a performance, so I will watch it on the television.' That is how it should be.

Michael Caine

MICHAEL CAINE, I seem to remember, was one of the
most difficult guests to pin down, simply because he is
usually filming in America. I spoke to him at the end of a long
series of highly successful films, *Educating Rita*, *Mona Lisa*,
Hannah and Her Sisters and *Sweet Liberty*.

One of the people's favourite actors, he received the Royal
seal of approval and appeared on the same show as Prince
Philip. Michael was able to break the news that he was leaving
Beverly Hills and coming back to live in England . . .

I hope I'm coming home for good. I decided I wanted to come
home and talk to people about the weather. You can't talk about
the weather in Los Angeles. You open the curtains and the sun's
shining. If you talked to a Los Angelean about the weather, he'd
think you were nuts. There's nothing to say. The sun shines. You
can't see it for the smog, but the sun is there. I thought I lived in the
countryside in Los Angeles which meant I lived on the top of a
Beverly Hill with the top sliced off and a house on it. You feel
you're in the country; there's rabbits and chipmunks and coyotes
and everything, but you're five minutes from Gucci's.

I thought the time had come to go home when I was watching an
English show one afternoon. One of these very uppercrust things
with French windows and everything, everybody saying 'Bunty's
having a party', and tennis shorts. I was sitting there and everybody seemed to be going 'Blah, blah, blah, blah,' and I thought to
myself I'd better go back to England because I didn't know what

the hell the people were talking about. It's true. I was trying to lipread, but of course their lips don't move. British people talk without moving their lips.

But seriously, one of the reasons I wanted to come back was for my daughter Natasha. She grew up for the first six years in England, and she would have been in America eight and a half years. She had a fabulous education – they're really wonderful – but I just wanted her to know something about England. I was talking to her one day and she said 'Everybody knows that World War Two started in 1941'. I said 'Darling, I think it's time to go back to England and maybe do a little English history.'

You hear hairy stories about American schools but that's only certain schools – Beverly Hills High is a very good name for it, I can tell you! But my daughter went to a Catholic school called Mary-mount. My wife's Muslim and I'm Protestant, so I decided to send her there. All her godparents are Jewish. She's going to get into heaven on a technicality, so to speak.

Now we are back in England and living in a small village. I grew up in Norfolk – I was evacuated – so I'm going back to my second childhood. I know practically everybody in the village. They don't see me as anything special. I sort of cycle up and down with Natasha the way they do. I've always got old clothes on. I'm extremely unostentatious. I don't drive some great Rolls or anything. I've read the lesson in church at Christmas. The vicar told me that was the biggest box office they'd ever had. I think if you're going to move into a small community you should join in.

I want to give Natasha the sort of upbringing where she's with the family all the time. I had a very happy childhood in a working class family. I always came home to my family, and it was a solid family. Every evening tea was ready – or somebody was there. I'm not hypocritical about boarding school. I have no right to be because I have no experience of it, except a lot of guys I meet who've been there and stutter.

Have you noticed the number of guys who stutter who go to boarding school? I think it's being dragged away from your Mum at nine. Then you're confronted with someone and they bark questions at you, and you start – 'wh-wh-wh-wh . . . where's my Mum?'

Mind you, the class system has broken down a lot but strangely I

136

think the greatest perpetuators of it are the working class. I'll give you a difference between America and Britain: Here I watch someone like a coalminer, who says 'They can't close the pit. I've been a miner and I want my son to be a miner.' In the United States a coal miner says 'I've been a miner all my life. I want my son to be a geologist.' There's the difference. And you can't put that over.

My father always said to me, 'I do a job carrying fish about. Never do a job where you can be replaced by a machine.' So I became an actor. And the first play I ever did, I played a robot! It was a Czechoslovakian, esoteric sort of play, called *Rossen's Universal Robots*, I played a robot, and a critic in the South London press said, 'As a robot, Mr Caine was very convincing.'

It's funny to look back on those early days in rep. I was Assistant Stage Manager and electrician and all that. And I used to do small parts. I did my own make-up, lipstick and everything, always a trifle heavy because of the lights. I looked like Greta Garbo or Boy George. I mean this was thirty years ago – when even girls didn't look like Boy George!

Times have changed, of course, since those days. Now I'm offered a lot of scripts – but very few of them are worth doing. Sometimes I choose a script because the location looks good. If the script starts off and it says 'Our hero walks on to the deck of the yacht as it pulls into San Tropez', I say I'll do it! If it says he comes screaming out of a blizzard at the South Pole, forget it! I did a picture last year, *Sweet Liberty*, with Alan Alda. Alan Alda said 'I've written this for you.' I said 'Really? What's the part?' He said 'A conceited old film star.' I said 'Where are you going to do it?' He said 'The Hamptons, in Long Island.' (Which is a great place.) And he said 'We've got you a house on the beach in June and July.' I said 'I'll do it.' And I had a great time. You see, I like to have my family with me. I like my daughter and my family to go where I go. Michael Caine is just a complete family man!

As Michael himself might have said – 'not a lot of people know that!'

137

Dynasty

Diahann Carroll

T HE THING about 'Dynasty', for a start, is that the
Americans can't pronounce it properly. 'Die-Nasty' for
Heaven's sake! Then there's the little ungrammatical faux pas
of '*La* Mirage', *zut alors*! There's even more big bucks flying
around Denver than Dallas, and a *lot* more shoulder-pads,
sex and chandeliers! And as for the names! Caress?! Kristal,
Fallon, Blake, Dex, Alexis . . . Dominique was the first to
crack and give us a peep over the bannisters.

DIAHANN: One of the papers said that I struggled for years
trying to become successful as a singer – I thought that was interesting. I've been quoted so many times, it's become a way of life. I
wake in the morning and say 'Well, what have they said about me
today?' In fact, I actually was called by Barbra Streisand because
she did a film called *Yentl*, and out of the film there was a lovely
song. She asked if I would perform this song in something we call
the Golden Globe. I agreed to do so. So I flew to Beverly Hills –
and I performed for the entire audience. I didn't realise that Aaron
Spelling, Esther Shapiro the creator of 'Dynasty' and her husband
Richard, and the producers, and Linda Evans and John Forsythe
and Joan Collins were all sitting there! That's how it happened.

WOGAN: Are you pleased with being Dominique?

DIAHANN: I couldn't be happier.

WOGAN: Not just for the money?

DIAHANN: The money has a great deal to do with it.

WOGAN: I thought it might. Isn't it very plucky really, by their standards, for the producers of 'Dynasty' to introduce, may we say, a token black person – not just that but a black person who is villainous?

DIAHANN: That's right. That was my entire requirement, that it was not token. Token means boring. I thought, either I'm a part of the major plot that goes on and I'm really literally connected to the Carringtons – I never expected them to make me related to the Carringtons. I'm very very happy with the role. It becomes more important as time goes on. I'm getting more ruthless, more powerful –

WOGAN: But they shot you.

DIAHANN: Ah! But have they?

WOGAN: I don't know. Let me examine you for flesh wounds. No, you appear to be unmarked. Mind you, it was only a superficial examination.

DIAHANN: You're a devil!

WOGAN: You must have felt something as those bullets surged through you?

DIAHANN: Actually, it was a very mild surging through me, because my contract had been signed –

WOGAN: So you're going to live! Who hasn't signed?

DIAHANN: You'll soon find out!

WOGAN: It's a tough business, isn't it?

DIAHANN: It is. But I love it. Even though I get up at three o'clock in the morning very often, in order to be in make-up at four o'clock. I'm having a wonderful time.

WOGAN: All the ladies on the show are so glamorous. Each new outfits stuns. They're terrible – they're a *bit* over the top.

DIAHANN: They're supposed to be. I think that's why you watch it. If you're going to see it walking up and down the street, why would you tune in at night? Everything is exaggerated, glamorous to the point of the ridiculous. And obviously you love it. That's why we do it. The audience says that it's wonderful that she's wearing mink sleeves and diamonds and having coffee in her office at twelve o'clock in the afternoon. Where else can you have that except on television!

John Forsythe

AND THEN hotfoot from the Carrington mansion, John Forsythe – a more sprightly figure in real life than old Blake:

JOHN FORSYTHE: I'm fortunate enough to be surrounded by lovely, lovely ladies, and they lavish every attention on me. Totally undeserved, I must say. Except I control the purse strings.

WOGAN: Do you really enjoy that part?

FORSYTHE: I enjoy playing love scenes with Linda Evans.

WOGAN: But a bit of a struggle getting past the old shoulder pads?

FORSYTHE: You know, those are not shoulder pads. There was a sequence in the thing where I was very upset with Krystal, shoulder pads and all. She came back into the house and I sat there brooding. It was because she had been taking birth control bills. I decided to do something about it. I decided I was going to show her who was the man in the household. So I threw her forcibly down on the bed and wrestled with her. Linda is a lady that does a lot of exercises. To wrestle this Viking woman down onto the bed and to hold her down there was a tremendous strain. For three or four days I was painfully sore. My wife said 'Why do you go round weeping and holding your arms?' I said 'Because I was wrestling Linda Evans'!

Each character we bring into the show represents some kind of

144

quality. She represents a sweet, dear, wonderful quality. She is the best-loved woman in the entire world. The best-looking wrestler as well. Joan represents something else. Evil incarnate. And I represent goodness. And sweetness.

Pamela Bellwood

I WAS LUCKY that Claudia spoke to me. The red carpet and car that she expected at the airport had not been ordered. A Carrington almost had to hitch a lift! But how did it begin for her?

I was with my husband and my stepson and we were camping in Death Valley. I think my career was at a fallow point. And the call came in to do the show. I was there on a party line –.everybody could listen in. And my agent was doing this negotiating. I was standing on a rattlesnake watch because there were rattlesnakes in the area. And my husband and son said to me, 'Don't do it, don't do it. You can do some more movies.' And we were riding around in a lot of rented camping equipment. I realised that we could just buy all this equipment if I just said yes. So I said yes on the party line, and everybody went 'Yeeeeah'.

From the beginning, I have been allowed to interpret the part, but I don't identify with her at all, not in the least. The instincts I've used to create her go on. Claudia has spent so much time crying I have no tear ducts left. They all dried up. I think I spent the first two years crying about my husband. They were alive then they were dead. There was no continuity in the show.

The trouble is now that no one really has a sense of humour or ever has any fun. I think, my goodness, what's the point of accumulating all this money if it just means suffering? Many times John Forsythe and I have thought we should just do a humorous version of 'Dynasty' because it *is* funny. I think the audience

146

doesn't really watch it to watch reality. They watch it because it's escapism. I think that's the element we've exported.

Incidentally, Terry, Diahann Carroll brought us a big bottle of laxative because she said you were calling the show 'Dysentry' – how could you?!

Stephanie Beacham

A S YOU may have noticed, things are not much different in 'Dynasty II – The Colbys'. Stephanie Beacham made, as we all noticed, a remarkable transition from her roles in *Tenko* and *Connie* to the character of Sable. Needless to say, she resisted the urge at first . . .

It all began when my agent phoned and said 'Will you come to London and do a test. They're going to do a "Dynasty II".' I said 'What? No. No way.' Then I phoned my next door neighbour to ask how my fish and my plants were doing. She said 'I've done the most terrible thing. I've left the key inside your house! I've locked your fish and plants up without food and water and I can't get in.' So, since I had to come up to London to feed the fish, I did the test to be kind to my agent. Then I got greedy – the rest you know.

I've just seen a playback of about episode four, and thought my goodness me, Sable is just a character in search of a hair-do – help! The idea is, we take her very near the edge – an unforgivable woman – and then we turn her over and show she's got a bit of vulnerability. When I started, I thought I was there to play the Alexis on 'Colbys'. But in fact, Sable's turning into a different sort of person altogether.

I have learned that all that's important on 'The Colbys' – or any soap – is whether the earrings are going to shine well enough, and whether your face is going to be well enough lit. But you don't do any of the internal rehearsal. Would you believe that any script changes have to be in 72 hours before? If you want to change an

148

'and' or a 'but' it's 72 hours before? You see, where they put their money in America is making sure that it looks good. And it does, even though I have to play a woman who's a frightful neurotic – she gets very upset if things don't go her way. In reality, I sometimes feel the urge to go over to the fireplace and burst into uncontrollable laughter!

I understand that Bungalow Bill Wiggins has just acquired an agent. It can only be a matter of time, then, before a charming adventurer knocks on Alexis's door . . .

Victor Mature

WHO WAS it that dared to come on the show wearing dark glasses and chewing gum, expecting to be recognised . . . Victor Mature, that's who.

I was seven years old when I first appeared on stage. I was watching a movie called *Over The Hills To The Poorhouse*. Mary Carr and Johnny Walker were playing in it, and Johnny Walker was the son and Mary Carr the mother. Johnny sent his poor old Mom to the poorhouse, and this I couldn't stand. I ran up on the stage, and hit the screen. That was my first stage appearance. And my father had to pay for the screen.

People think of me as always wearing togas or fighting lions. I really had to fight them for some shots. No matter how many stuntmen you have, you have to do some close shots. De Mille asked me one day 'I'd like you to get very close, Victor, to this lion. Very close.' I said 'How close?' He said 'Right up to its mouth as if you wanted to bite it.' I said 'Mr. De Mille, you'd better hire yourself another boy. I don't want to get that close to that lion.' He said 'Don't worry. This lion has no teeth.' I said, 'Mr. De Mille, I don't even want to be gummed.'

Another thing people remember is my tearing down the temple in *Samson and Delilah*. Everyone's seen that movie. You saw me pushing the two pillars apart, looking very strong. Let me tell you a secret. You know those hydraulic things in the garage, where your car goes up and down? Each one of those pillars had those hydraulic things inside them. I just got between, gave a little push and the whole town fell in. Sorry to ruin the illusion.

My next movie is with Sylvester Stallone. He called me last week and asked me if I would consider playing his father. I said 'Sylvester, if the price is right, I'll play your mother.'

These days I play a lot of golf. In fact when I started to play golf a lot I went to join the L.A. country club. I walked in and asked the manager if I could join. He said 'We cannot accept you, Mr. Mature, because you're an actor.' I said 'Because I'm an *actor*? That's the reason I can't get in?' I said 'Well that won't keep me out. I've got 36 films I could run for you and the 36 reviews to prove it.'

John Mortimer

THE WRITER and barrister John Mortimer always makes for excellent conversation. He is the master of witty dissidence and sardonic protest. Last time he dropped in, he gave another insight into the inner secrets of the creator of *Rumpole of the Bailey*.

I enjoy champagne and I enjoy the company of women. I'm a champagne socialist. Or I'm a Bollinger Bolshevik. I see absolutely no reason why champagne should be confined to Dennis Thatcher, or people who vote Conservative, or even members of the SDP. Champagne should be made freely available to the public.

My idea of perpetual damnation on the other hand is, I think, an all-male dinner at the Institute of Chartered Accountants.

The thing about my profession, the law, is that both barristers and criminals are extremely male chauvinistic, and your average decent, hard-working British bank robber thinks that men should rob the banks, and that women should stay at home and look after the children. And they think that women committing crimes is really rather disgusting. So on the whole they prefer to be defended by men, because they think that barristers' wives or lady barristers should be at home looking after the children.

But I always found women on juries were very sensible. And in particular if you did the sort of cases I did for a while, which I used to call cases about the liberty of the subject and defending free speech – other people used to call them dirty book cases – women

152

on the jury were invaluable because they weren't particularly emotionally involved in those sorts of publications. Whereas the men got extremely hot under the collar, over-excited, thumbed over the exhibits eternally because they wanted to do the things they had done. I think that women are practical, sensible, down-to-earth, rational. I think men are creatures of fantasy. They're emotionally, incredible butterflies.

What we have to cope with in England, though, is the art of understatement between men and women. I think the English are very emotional underneath all that understatement – which is what makes it a wonderful thing to write about. Because what you must always do with English dialogue is to suggest what people are thinking without them saying it. They're always saying something different. When they're saying 'Pass the tea' they really mean 'I've fallen passionately in love with you, darling. Two sugars please.'

And finally, to dispel more illusions, I have to tell you, I went on a pilgrimage to Canterbury Cathedral on Friday with a nun and a knight in a Rolls Royce. So now I'm not only a champagne social-ist, I'm a Rolls Royce pilgrim.

Lord Denning

IT WAS my pleasure to welcome on to the show one evening one of the great men of British public life – a man who can claim to be the longest-serving judge in history. For 38 years he adjudicated, and often he was outspoken on legal matters. Nowadays, judges have to retire at 75, but Lord Denning carried on way past that. When I met him he was as bright as a button at 83.

LORD DENNING: I like my work, and I was fond of it. But I was getting a bit old, you know, 83. I'm still carrying on though. I still go to the House of Lords now, you know. People sometimes think we're asleep when they see us in the House of Lords, but what really happens is we're leaning back because there's a loud-speaker at the end of each seat. So we're really listening . . . It's different from the House of Commons, you know. They start the proceedings with prayer. The chaplain looks at the assembled members with their varied intelligence, and then prays for the country!

WOGAN: Spending all those years in the law – many people still refer to the law as an ass. What's your view of it?

DENNING: Mr. Bumble says 'The law's an ass.' He said that because the law said the man coerced his woman, or the other way about. The law is not an ass, at all events when I try and enunciate it. They said I used to change the law when I was Master of the Rolls. Well, a student wrote to *The Times* newspaper and they printed it saying, 'Sir, with respect to the Master of the Rolls, will his Lordship kindly refrain from changing any more laws before the law examinations in August'.

Not everyone, I suppose, knows what the Master of the Rolls is. I can tell you a true story about a letter I had from International Students House in London, and this is what it said. 'Dear Lord Denning, I am an Indian citizen. I graduated in mechanical engineering in the University of London, and was awarded a Master of Science degree. I feel I have the necessary qualifications, motivation, energy, drive and personality to begin a successful career in an automobile industry. I will ever remain grateful to you if you can kindly help me to begin my professional career with your company, The Rolls Royce Motor Company.'

WOGAN: Sometimes it appears when your Lordships are delivering judgements, you're not entirely in touch with reality. One remembers the judge who asked 'Who are the Beatles?'

DENNING: Sometimes they say 'Who's Terry Wogan?'

WOGAN: Quite right. But you will agree judges sometimes seem a little out of touch?

DENNING: I don't agree, no. Some people think that judges all come from the upper class. That's all nonsense. Judges come from every class. My father was a small draper. Lots of judges come from every class. They mix with everyone. It's quite wrong to think that the judges are out of touch. The judges are really first rate. I'll speak up for them. Although I didn't always agree with others, you know. I always said that when I was a judge alone, I could and did do justice. But in the Court of Appeal of three, I found the chances of doing justice were two to one against!

WOGAN: Have you had doubts about whether you were ever right or wrong?

DENNING: I think it's right to say this: often I would be in difficulty, but as long as I did what I thought was right, I'd be happy and sleep o' nights. But if I had doubts and I asked myself was I right or wrong, I wouldn't sleep. I'd be too anxious. No, I think as long as I felt I did what was right, I was quite happy and content.

WOGAN: Do you remember your first brief?

DENNING: Yes. It was a little brief, I think for about two guineas, down at the Greenwich County Court. I took the train at Charing Cross, made sure it was the right train, and lo and behold, it rushed through Greenwich, straight on. I pulled the communication cord. And it went on for a whole mile, then it stopped. The guard was annoyed. I scrambled down the embankment, and got to my case. And afterwards those railway solicitors wrote to me and they threatened to prosecute me and have the penalty of £5. But I talked them out of it!

WOGAN: Do you think it's a good idea that judges should be allowed to speak out of court?

DENNING: Oh, you're thinking of someone who's getting on the television, is it? Or the radio. It's *not* a good thing unless you have a really good chap like me! No, actually, it is unwise for a serving judge, because there is a danger of his commenting on pending cases or expressing a view on cases which may come before him. On the whole, it's not a wise thing to do and rules have been laid down for it. But you mustn't think I'm casting any reflection on anyone now. I've got to be careful about the law of libel and slander and all that. I think on the whole it's wise for a serving judge to keep off television.

WOGAN: Finally, what's your sport – football or cricket?

DENNING: Cricket. I'm patron of the Hampshire County Cricket Club. Do you know the schoolboys' definition of the game of cricket? You have two sides, one out in the field, one in. Each man on the field that's out goes in, and when he's out, he comes in, and the next man goes in until he's out. When they're all out the side that's been out in the field comes in, and the side that was in goes out, and tries to get those coming in out. When they're all out, including the not outs, that's the end of the game.

HRH
the Prince Philip

W HEN I invited Prince Philip on to 'Wogan', he had
one thing on his mind – carriage driving – a sport
which you would be totally forgiven for knowing absolutely
nothing about. It was relatively new even to the Prince as he
was to admit. I could see a sporting interview in the offing but
I began by asking what had happened to the sport I had long
associated with Prince Philip – the sport of kings, polo?

I suppose it's always a bit sad to find that age is catching up with
you. But I'd made up my mind some five years before that I was
going to give up polo when I was fifty. Or if anything broke in the
meantime. Fortunately my wrist went bad, and my ponies went
bad, and I was fifty, all at the same time. I reckoned that was a
good moment to stop. Polo takes place at quite a high speed. It's
rather athletic and there comes a time in your life when you don't
want to be quite so athletic any more, I can tell you.

*Prince Charles still plays polo. So had the Duke been a better
player?*

It's not for me to decide. There is a thing called the handicap
committee, and they decide what handicap you should have. In
this country, it's between minus two and plus ten. Well, we've got
some plus eights and nines. I got up to five. I'd been playing longer

157

than he had when I got to five. He may make it yet. He's still young and vigorous. He's younger than I am, funnily enough, though he may not look it. No, that was unkind, I didn't mean that! I thought you were going to talk about the carriage driving.

Suitably chastised I enquired further about this strange, new passion.

I've done strange things. I was invited to become the President of the International Equestrian Federation, which is one of these governing bodies for international sport. Somebody came along to me one day and said 'You know, we ought to have international rules for carriage driving.' I said 'I've never heard of it.' And then I took a bit of interest, and found that it was quite popular in Germany and in Hungary particularly. And so I asked one of the great sort of horse people in this country to chair the committee and to write some rules. He came up with this idea of providing rules for carriage driving competition based on the three-day event. He drafted the rules, and of course I got my fingers on to them, edited them – I didn't change them, just edited them.

It's funny, you know; I now find it addictive. Once you've got your eye in, you can see an awful lot, what the bloke's like or the horses are like, the whole sort of atmosphere. You can see it in those ten minutes much more clearly than you could see it at any other time. It's certainly not boring. You feel rather like some Bishop said when making an after dinner speech, like a swan, all serene and calm on the surface, and paddling like hell underneath.

There's really a huge spread of competitor and they come from all over, all kinds and backgrounds. Horses are great levellers. There are people from the Army, there are farmers, there's a plant hire man who sponsors himself, there's a scrap metal merchant, I think from Penrith. You can usually tell the drivers – they're all shoulders and no legs!

Anybody can fall off a carriage and roll one over! But it's not particularly dangerous. Things happen, but they're seldom serious. I've turned the carriage over two or three times and I've been bounced off it occasionally, because the going's a bit rough. I

158

claim to have, I think, almost the record. In the very first club competition of the season, at the very first obstacle, I went into it and hit a post or something and turned the carriage over, righted the thing, went out, and went back to do the thing properly. I went in and turned it over the other way. I think I must be one of the only competitors to have ever turned over twice at the same obstacle.

But what about the cost of this strange sport?

It's less expensive than you think because they use the horses out of the mews, the ones they use for all these State occasions. My horses were in the last wedding. When I came back from St.Paul's, I was with the bride's mother, and the two horses that were pulling me were two of the horses that normally pull me in these competitions. They were being driven by my coachman who normally stands on the back and gives me advice. So it was the other way round. I was giving him advice.

Finally, I wondered if Her Majesty the Queen had ever travelled as a passenger with Prince Philip – and if she shouted instructions?

Not when I'm driving horses, but when I'm driving cars I get it.

Simon Weston

SIMON WESTON was one of the bravest men I have ever met. A member of the Welsh Guards, he was extremely badly injured in the *Sir Galahad* bombing during the Falklands War. On the day I met him, he had just been elected a Man of the Year and had been through a dozen operations to repair his face and hands which had literally melted in the intense heat of the flames.

He might not have come on to the show had it not been for his mother who dragged him into the theatre and sat with him in hospitality. Simon told me how strong she was: 'she can almost cut toast with her breath!' With great dignity, he told what had happened to him since that fateful day.

When the bomb went off, I didn't actually feel anything. I felt I was swallowing a lot of heat. I saw a lot of horrific things on board the *Sir Galahad*. But I didn't actually feel any pain. I felt a lot of hot smoke as it went down my throat, but I didn't actually feel any pain till I came up on top. Then when they cut my trousers off, I could feel the cold air on me.

The flame and flash had burnt all the nerve endings away, so I couldn't feel anything at the time. My trousers protected me, to an extent, but my legs were still burnt. When I got up on top deck they cut my trousers off and the cold air – I could feel it then because not all the nerve endings had been burnt away in the legs.

I've never felt bitter about what happened. I suppose everybody who gets hurt and injured says 'Why me?' But I've never been bitter about it. It was a job that everybody has to do – well, every soldier has to do. And unfortunately, war is not glory. It definitely is not a glorious thing.

I joined the army at sixteen. I joined the Welsh Guards. I joined to get some discipline, really. I was a bit wild when I was young. I didn't see there was anything I really wanted to do when I left school.

I suppose no soldier would ever join an army if he ever thought he was going to be hit by a bullet. You always assume it's going to be someone else. I did think at the time, 'Why me?' But I think that's a natural reaction. I've felt angry about certain things. I don't think anyone could love the man who does something like this to them. But I wouldn't hate the man. He only did to me what, if I'd had the chance, I'd have done to him. A soldier that gets injured at war knows he's actually doing his job and he knows his job is to kill or be killed, injure or be injured, maim or be maimed.

Where I live, the people in the village have been fantastic, and I've been supported by a lot of people all over the country as well. People do look at me. You can't avoid some of the stares or glares. But most of the time you just ignore them. I think I've come to learn to live with it to a great extent.

But although I'm hurt on the outside, I'm quite rich on the inside, really. Because I've come through it and I've had lots of support, and I've seen there's a lot more good in this world than there is bad. People should try not to knock it so much. And try not to knock so many people so much. There's a lot of people trying to do a lot of good. There's too many people trying to criticise too quickly, without seeing the effort that's put into the back of it.

The worst period for me was coming out of hospital after the first operation. After all the fuss had died away, I went into a depression, which was very hard. I drank quite heavily, and became very aggressive. But it was delayed depression, really. I didn't feel I could talk to anybody, and didn't feel there was anybody who knew what I was going through. But there's always somebody. And then the Welsh Guards came along to me and they said, 'Do you want to go back to the Regiment to watch a game of rugby with the friends you used to play with?' And they took me back, paid for the flight and everything. And from that day on, I've never really looked back. Now I go back to the Welsh Guards as often as I can.

I'm only 24 so there's so much more to do and to see in life. I don't think it ever really stops you if you want to do something. There's a lot of people who have been injured a lot longer than I have who have achieved great heights and are still achieving them, so there's a lot of scope for me yet.

George Best

A S FAR as sportsmen go, George Best has rarely left the
public eye – but not always because of his skill on the
field. By common consent he was the outstanding footballer
of his generation. He was British and European Footballer of
the Year at the age of 22 and an international at 18. But when
he came on 'Wogan' in 1986, it was after a period when all
had gone terribly wrong for him – and he had just been
released from prison. His fall from grace has been well
documented by the popular press. His appearance was the
first time he had spoken publicly after his release. He had
ceased to be 'prisoner M76245', and I was able to welcome
back the man, looking remarkably fit:

Funnily enough, prison was quite enjoyable. The nice thing was,
the first day I got there, one of the inmates came up to me and said
'You'll be OK in here because you've done two things we all want
to do. You got drunk and got caught, and you shinned a police-
man. We'll take care of you.'

The thing was, I did something wrong, and I was punished for it,
but really once I got in there I put my head down and decided I had
to get through it. I made the most of it even though I was locked up
23 hours a day, which isn't fun under any circumstances, even less
when you have to do it in a prison.

It was good from the point of view that I found out a lot of things
about myself. Not only that. While I was there I received something like seven thousand cards from well-wishers. I got the odd

163

one or two from a crank, but the nice thing was that seven thousand had found time to write to me, and say they hoped I got over it, and things would be OK. Seven thousand people don't write to you if you're a hundred per cent bad. It made me feel good.

The reason I fell, as it were, was because of drink. I am one of millions of people round the world who suffer from what is a disease called alcoholism. I think the sooner people realise that it is a disease the better it is going to be. It took a long time to recognise that I had a disease, or maybe I didn't want to admit it. I didn't want to say that I couldn't just have one drink and leave it at that. I couldn't. It affects me differently, in my system. Sadly, it didn't only affect me but the people close to me.

I don't want to reform, because I'm having a great time. The only thing I'm going to change is to stop drinking because it affects my personality and it hurts a lot of people. I will have a hell of a fight every day just to stop myself from drinking. That'll be there for ever. But I'm not going to lock myself away. I don't want to become a recluse. I don't want to end up like Howard Hughes. I still enjoy the good things in life. And if I keep working at the one thing, I think I'm going to make it.

Kirk Douglas

THE MOVIE greats ... they are getting fewer all the time, and so I was particularly pleased to welcome the star of *The Vikings*, *Champion*, and *Lust for Life*, Kirk Douglas, on to 'Wogan'. The man with the famous dimple in the chin. Meeting him in real life, you would never believe that he has made a living for all these years out of playing some of the most unsavoury characters on screen. I found him an unaffected man and I was very pleased that he was also slightly smaller than me!

In many ways, I consider myself to be a failure, because I did not attain in life what I set out to do. My aim in life was to be a star on the Broadway stage. Well, I never became a star on the Broadway stage. I did about twelve Broadway shows. I was quite consistent, most of them were flops.

I flopped on Broadway but I kept going back. The last time I was there, I did the play *One Flew Over the Cuckoo's Nest*. I bought the book, I did the play for five, six months and took no salary because I thought it was a wonderful play. The critics didn't know quite how to take it. For almost twelve years I tried to make a movie out of it. But finally my son, Michael, said 'Dad, let me try'. We became partners, and, of course, he made the movie. It was a huge success. I said to him 'I don't mind you making all that money, but what I do mind is that I didn't get to play that part. Not only did Jack Nicholson play it, but he played it so well.' That really bothered me!

I was never encouraged to be an actor. In fact, when I was a child there was no such thing as encouragement. My parents were illiterate immigrants. They came from Russia. My going to university, working my way through school, was a foreign thing. It was all new to them. It wasn't a question of ever encouraging me. It was a question of survival.

I think I had the *advantage* of being born in abject poverty. If my father had had a certain amount of money, I don't know what I would have become. The fact that my four sons who were born into a certain amount of affluence are all functioning well, I think, is a tribute to them.

I gave my sons lots of advice. I told all four of them never to go into show business. All of them went into show business. So I think that's one of the ways, if you want your sons to do something, you say 'You mustn't do this'.

But show business is something like an incurable disease. I think it's pathetic. It's poignant, sad. The chances of success are remote. For every person that becomes successful, there are thousands who have tried and haven't succeeded. You want to spare your children that rejection. The rejection of an actor is a very personal one. If you write a book, you say 'This is a book I wrote' or if you paint a picture you say 'This is a picture, do you like the picture I painted?' But an actor is saying 'Do you like me?' And if they say no, that's a personal rejection. It's painful.

I also think that acting is really a childish profession when you think about it. Imagine a grown-up man like me pretending to shoot it out with Burt Lancaster! You have to retain a certain naivety or you couldn't do it.

The most difficult thing for me now is trying to be myself. I find that it's much easier to hide behind a character that I'm playing, to have a director direct me, or to have the lines that a writer has written for me. Then I feel comfortable. I think that's another form of escape. You may not know it, but I am a very shy person!

I suppose the part that really established me was playing a tough boxer in a film called *Champion*. It stamped me as a tough guy. Before that I played weak alcoholics, or I played intellectual schoolteachers. But after *Champion* people began to recognise me.

One day soon after it was released, I went into a bar. I thought

166

I'd have a quick beer, and I stood at the bar and saw people sort of noticing me. There were two or three tough-looking guys sitting in a booth. They watched me, and I saw them mumbling to each other. One guy got up and he started to walk across toward me and I thought 'Oh my, now what's going to happen?' When he came halfway across, I slammed my fist on the bar, and everybody turned and looked at me, and I said 'Anybody in this bar can lick me.' Everybody laughed, the guy lost interest and went back to his seat.

I've never shied away from playing an unsavoury character. I think virtue is not so photogenic. Bad guys are more interesting. It's difficult, because I really am a nice, clean-cut fellow. But so many of the parts that I find interesting to play very often are characters that are unsavoury.

There were a few exceptions – I played Van Gogh, the artist, in *Lust for Life*. John Wayne saw the film and said, 'Why did you play a snivelling, weak painter?' I said, 'Come on, John, I'm an actor. I'm trying to play a role.' He said, 'No. People like you and I have got to play macho guys.' I said, 'Wait a minute. You're really not John Wayne.' And he was literally very annoyed. He felt I was not true to my class. You see, some actors develop an image they like to cling to. I think the public has imposed an image on me.

I was nominated for an Oscar for *Lust for Life*. But I never won an Oscar. I was nominated a few times, but I never won. Each time that I was nominated I prepared a beautiful acceptance speech. I never got a chance to use it!

I like to think that as you get more mature – rather than use that word old – you learn a lot of things. You develop a sense of values. I think all of life is learning something, getting to know more, developing a better set of values. Especially now.

When I look at my son Michael and see the tremendous success he's attained, I think to myself, I should have been much nicer to him when he was young. I didn't know he was going to do so well. What I like to do is to be working with my four sons. Joe producing, Peter directing, Michael and Eric and I acting. You always have to have dreams in life, no matter how old you are. Browning said it in a poem. 'A man's reach should far exceed his grasp, else what's a heaven for?' I think you always have to have something you're striving for.

Fanny Cradock

O NE OF the most memorable and dramatic encounters I
 had ever had on 'Wogan', and an interview that I shall
never forget, was with that maitresse of the cuisine . . .
Fanny Cradock. She was desperate to tell me about Edward
and Mrs. Simpson. I wanted to know about her life with
Johnnie and their time as television cooks. Never known for
understatements or reticence, she had bullied and harried the
great British public into better home cooking. She knocked
seven bells out of me while she was at it!

FANNY CRADOCK: I'm glad to be here. The first television
we ever did was in this theatre, Johnnie and I together. Half an
hour. Invited audience. We were so scared. Johnnie was kicked in
the small of the back to go on. He said 'Go on, Johnnie, you silly
old b . . ., you're on'. And he lurched onto television.

WOGAN: Now Fanny, you've brought me a little something to
taste.

FANNY: That's for the end of the programme, you gutsy.

WOGAN: Am I expected to talk to you without eating here?

FANNY: Oh all right. They are raspberry puffballs – I know
what a sweet tooth you've got. They're outrageous for the figure.

WOGAN: Luckily I don't have to worry.

FANNY: Yes, you're so slim. Can you see over the top of your
tum still?

WOGAN: There's not much to see over the top of my tum. For over twenty years you were the maitresse of cuisine, weren't you? That marvellous style of teaching people how to cook. The Queen Mother complimented you, didn't she?

FANNY: Yes, at the end of an interview, she asked 'In your opinion has the standard of cooking improved in this country?' And both Johnnie and I enthusiastically said 'Oh, enormously.' And we dried, because she turned with that inimitable smile of hers and said 'Yes, and in our opinion you're responsible for it.' And we stood there like a couple of codfish and forgot to bow or curtsey.

WOGAN: Do you think that cooks are born? Rather than made?

FANNY: No. I think there's a feeling for food, a feeling for cookery, which is an impetus. You know that expression, you know damn well you're in for a damned bad meal with a lazy cook. But you can make any woman cook.

WOGAN: How about a feller? It's not just women's work, surely?

FANNY: No, but I'm more interested in women in cooking. It's the absolute hub of the home. I think if you can't cook, you're a rotten wife. But just to be on the safe side, for when I was ill or in bed, or anything else, I taught John to cook.

WOGAN: Now you used to prepare quite elaborate dishes. Women don't have time. In *your* time . . .

FANNY: Enough of this 'in your time'. I'm not dead yet. There's plenty of life in me. And I'm coming back to cook some more on television. So there.

WOGAN: But I mean women don't have time for elaborate dishes, do they?

FANNY: If this is one of your devious little work-rounds to convenience food, I'll tell you straight out. There is only one convenience in convenience food and that is the profit for the manufacturers – and it's a load of muck.

169

WOGAN: What about nouvelle cuisine then?

FANNY: What about it?

WOGAN: Sorry I mentioned it.

FANNY: I should think so. When are we going to get off cooking and talk about my new book?

WOGAN: Whenever you like.

FANNY: Let's do it now. I wrote it five years ago. And I couldn't publish it. It's about Edward and Mrs. Simpson but it's not nice to the Duchess of Windsor and I had to wait until she was dead. It's the only time in my life I've ever waited for a dead anybody's shoes. What started me thinking about it was George Bernard Shaw and Mrs. Patrick Campbell. Do you remember when she suggested they had a baby together? He said 'No, dear. It's too risky. You suggest it might have your beauty and my brains. But suppose it was the other way around?' I thought, now there's enormous scope in this.

WOGAN: You honestly don't care much about people's feelings, do you? I know you're a great chum of Barbara Cartland, but sometimes you haven't been all that kind.

FANNY: Barbara? One of my best friends. Splendid woman. A bit overdone, but then so am I.

WOGAN: Is your book about the Duke and Duchess of Windsor a novel, or is it the truth?

FANNY: Find out by reading it.

WOGAN: Did you know Edward and Mrs. Simpson?

FANNY: Oh, yes. Mrs. Simpson, I think, was a perfectly ordinary simple prototype of an adventuress. Of the most acquisitive kind. David Windsor I adored, from the time I was a schoolgirl, when I first danced with him at a ball. He was so tight I held him up. He had his head over my shoulder. And he said to me 'You've got the most beautiful brown eyes I've ever seen in my life', and he couldn't see.

170

WOGAN: You've written over twenty books in what is a very active life.

FANNY: I've done nothing of the sort. I have written 104 and I'm on the 105th and 106th at the moment. Of them, there were 24 novels.

WOGAN: Another blunder.

FANNY: That's right. It doesn't worry me, and it doesn't worry you.

WOGAN: Now you're also writing a soap opera. For goodness' sake, give other people a chance.

FANNY: They've had plenty of chance to do a soap opera. In England. Bulging with glamour. I'm going to have a go at it.

WOGAN: Finally, you and Johnnie have been together now for fifty years?

FANNY: That's a very rude English type question. Which I will not answer. Only Englishmen go on about your age . . .

WOGAN: Let me rephrase that. You and Johnnie have been together now for a couple of years. What is your recipe for a happy marriage?

FANNY: I don't know. Good food. Super food. Children. I don't know, my dear. If I knew – if anybody knew the recipe for a happy marriage – there would be no divorce courts. It is a fusion of two people who can cope with the problems and find infinite solace, pleasure, and comfort in the best bit.

And after that I needed the raspberry puffballs!

Peter Ustinov

N O ONE in the world should, or could, consider starting a chat-show without first confirming that Peter Ustinov would be available at some time in the future. The man, as better interviewers than I will testify over the years, is pure gold. As a raconteur, a linguist, a mimic, a comedian, Ustinov has few equals. Polyglot, polymath, Polly put the kettle on, we'll all have tea and listen to a childhood fantasy . . .

One of my earliest memories was being a car. My parents were unbearably Bohemian. They never had a car of their own, and they never had a radio, so I became a radio before that. Then I graduated to being a car. Which worried my father more because I never spoke. I just switched myself on in the morning, drove around all day, hooting, and then at night I backed myself into bed, taking great care not to scratch the paintwork, and when I felt sleepy enough, switched off. My father worried because I never talked. One day I came out with quite a complicated sentence, and he was reassured. But he had a year and a half of agony. I've been talking fairly fully ever since.

My whole education is a dreadful memory for me. It was having to walk through a slum every morning dressed with a top hat and a tailed coat and we had to carry umbrellas to distinguish us from the City of London bank messengers. Who were dressed exactly as we were but didn't have umbrellas and were nearly all eighty years old. There was only one day more humiliating than the ones with the top hat. And they were the days we were in military uniform. I could never do my puttees up, and there's nothing worse than being stuck in the street at the age of thirteen carrying all your school books and an old military man helping you with your puttees, by kneeling in front of you in the street . . .

When I was a child, I heard as much German as English. I picked it up because my father was a newspaper correspondent here and when I was tiny he used to have to dictate at dictation speed all his reports – that was in 1924-5. And I heard it through the wall. It was like a record. It was snail's-pace – so I learned all the long words through insomnia. Only 'ja' and 'nein' came much later. I never heard those.

My fluency in German didn't always help during the last war. Once we were asked to 'take' the town of Maidstone which was to be defended by the Home Guard. I dropped out of the normal troops, and hatched the clever scheme whereby I knocked on people's doors and they came in pyjamas and said 'Yes?'. I said 'It's a military manoeuvre.' They said 'Oh yes, come in, what do you want?' 'I want to go through your garden.' I went through the back, out into their garden, into the back of the next house, knocked on the back windows and people came out in nightshirts. 'Yes?' 'Can I go through to your front door?' 'Why?' 'This is a military manoeuvre.' And so on. And I went right across Maidstone, never appearing in the streets. Going through it against the stream of traffic as it were.

I got to the middle of Maidstone, and I saw the enemy commander. I levelled my rifle and said 'Bang!' which was the only thing I could do. I informed him he was dead. And he refused to die, which was very bad form. He said 'How dare you come in here, unheralded?' And the umpire was a man with a very bad stutter, a second lieutenant, and he said 'I'm afraid y-you are d- . . .' and the General said 'I'm not!' Very ungraceful, not waiting for the poor man to finish. And he refused to die.

I was taken prisoner. I said 'This is most unfair.' And they asked me a lot of questions, and I said, 'Wait a minute, am I a prisoner, or dead?' They said 'Don't ask impertinent questions.' I said 'Very well. I'm a prisoner then.' They started reading personal letters and all sorts of things like that. Then they said 'How strong was your unit?' I said 'Ich habe mein Nummer und mein Namen gegeben.' They said 'What are you talking about?' While they weren't looking, I'd seized all their maps and trampled on them, and spilt ink on them, so I was seized by many men and put in the guardroom, which was also the armoury, full of rifles and things. They were absolutely furious that I wouldn't answer any questions except in German. And I was put under arrest. I seized a rifle and threatened them, and eventually had the most awful set-to.

My own Colonel arrived and said 'They want you arrested, but what have you done?' I said, 'Answered in German.' 'Was that wise?' I said, 'But sir, I thought this was us trying to capture Maidstone! I'm supposed to be German, aren't I?' He said, 'Yes, but you musn't carry things too far.' I said, 'You expect the Germans to call here and to talk in English?' He said, 'Well, personally I don't expect the Germans to come here at all.' I said, 'Then what are we doing here?' He said, 'Ha ha ha. All right, cut off back to your unit. Very amusing!' And that's the way the thing ended.

It didn't leave me with too high an opinion of the British officer. And that has continued to this day. I've nothing against officers – they were very courageous very often. But it's that kind of attitude. I remember that, because we were sent to Dover. We were the nearest point to German-occupied territory. The British built a ditch right across England as the first line of defence. This was very secret at the time. But I remember that as they were digging the ditch, the Governor of Dover Castle said through a megaphone, 'Not across the cricket pitch.' And that's where the Germans would have streamed through. That's gospel truth! I think enough time has passed now that I can release some of these plans, without risking persecution.

I remember another officer: at the moment of the first General Election after the war, I was in Bentley Priory beginning to do a film about radar. And they asked for complete silence because they wanted to hear the latest election results. And it came through. It said something like, 'Conservative 132, Labour 186'. So Labour were winning. And there was a ghastly silence. Then one RAF officer with a huge moustache said 'Try the Forces programme.'

Epilogue

And so, another 'Wogan' comes to its usually abrupt close. The floor manager sinks senseless to the ground, exhausted from 35 minutes of manic signalling and drained by the incessant shrieking of directors and producers in her head-phones. The audience sit bemused, waiting for the entertainment to start. They are astounded to learn that it's all over, when all they've seen is a frantic scurrying of machinery and the back of cameramen's heads. They exit into the roseate glow of a Shepherd's Bush evening, clambering aboard their charabancs and thence to Wales, Shropshire or Teesside, sighing dispiritedly and muttering darkly about licence fees and complaining to the Ombudsman.

Meanwhile, up in 'Hospitality', or as it's more accurately called in this book, 'Hostility', all is sophisticated bonhomie. Fine wines and viands, specially delivered by the Queen's own victuallers, are served discreetly by liveried butlers on spotless napery to the host and his guests. As they pick at foie gras and caviar, salmon and chateaubriand, the talk is of philosophy or the sciences, politics or religion. Many times a political head has rolled, a bishop's mitre changed hands, or the groves of academe been shaken, over the brandy and cigars. Occasionally, a head of state, or a passing prelate drops discreetly by; and – if he has made sure to clear it with the Great Man Himself – a place can sometimes be found for the D.G., bless him.

As night falls the limousines pull noiselessly away from the old theatre. All is silent on the green, save for the hoot of the owl and the cry of the vixen. Shepherd's Bush seems to hold its breath, in anticipation of another day, another 'Wogan' . . . Requiescat in pace . . .